AMERICAN DISSIDENT

AMERICAN DISSIDENT

ALEXANDER GUNN

Outskirts Press, Inc.
Denver, Colorado

American Dissident
Save Our Society
All Rights Reserved.
Copyright © 2011 Alexander Gunn
v2.0

Outskirts Press, Inc.
http://www.outskirtspress.com

ISBN: 978-1-4327-6812-6

Outskirts Press and the "OP" logo are trademarks belonging to Outskirts Press, Inc.

PRINTED IN THE UNITED STATES OF AMERICA

AMERICAN DISSIDENT

ALEXANDER GUNN

Outskirts Press, Inc.
Denver, Colorado

Outskirts Press, Inc.
http://www.outskirtspress.com

ISBN: 978-1-4327-6812-6

Outskirts Press and the "OP" logo are trademarks belonging to Outskirts Press, Inc.

PRINTED IN THE UNITED STATES OF AMERICA

Acknowledgments

This book is dedicated to the working men and women of America. The future can be brighter.

Special thanks to my family, Adriana, Richard, Luba, Guy, Joy, Igor, Demet and Patrick.

Cover art by Anna Torzillo. 2010

Contents

Introduction

Our precious democracy is threatened by incompetence and our will is being ignored. The major political parties have become little more than lackeys for the idle rich and multi-national corporations. Both parties are guilty of selling out the American worker to benefit Wall Street and free trade fraud. NAFTA and CAFTA are assaults on our wages and unions. Our government and corporations are in love with Communist China, kow-towing to unelected thugs who are responsible for a dismal human rights record. Both parties are guilty of wishy-washy border security and touchy-feely legislation for the "rights" of illegal aliens.

Books have been written about the struggle of the American working classes and incompetent government, but all too often, they are written by elitist, self-proclaimed experts who don't understand the daily challenge of working for a living. Should anyone really expect a media mogul, former governor or multi-millionaire to take the interests of workers seriously? Misguided globalists and open borders advocates do not speak for the American worker. They are apologists for corporations, assuring us that the future will be brighter if we keep auctioning off American jobs to the lowest foreign bidder and grant amnesty to more hordes of illegal aliens.

Should we automatically believe statistics and hype about our economy being healthy, robust and expanding? According to our government and Wall Street, we are still living in paradise. But pompous claims are no match for the raw reality in our country. Millions of our citizens suffer near or below the official government poverty line, a line set absurdly low to begin with. Real wages have steadily declined since the 1970s and decent manufacturing jobs have been eliminated here and sent to Asia and Mexico. Our workers feel less secure on the job, knowing they can be replaced (for any reason) with a temporary worker or immigrant.

Despite the offshoring of good jobs, we are

told (especially near election time) about the creation of millions of new jobs. But we must look closely and understand what kinds of jobs have been created to replace those lost to NAFTA, China and India. Service and temporary jobs have indeed been added to the economy, but these offer little or no *career* growth with wages that can not meet basic financial needs, unless you want to work two or three of them. All too often, higher positions are reserved for friends and family of the company founder and top management, or they're untouchable without a four year degree; when in reality, the job could be learned and mastered by a high school graduate with training and experience. Office politics and nepotism should never outweigh merit.

Millions of Americans simply don't make enough money to enjoy decent lives with modern conveniences as it is, but like a hungry vulture, the government descends on the thin wallets of the working classes with never-ending federal, state, gasoline, alcohol, tobacco and sales taxes to finance bloated programs, tax breaks for the inheriting class and foreign aid handouts.

Many Americans are frustrated with their government and have little faith in it, but people are also busy with their job(s) and families and there is uncertainty about who is really to blame. Is it the Democratic Party or the Republican Party? Both parties point fingers at each other so is a third *major* party needed? We have the right to demand improvement when our government and economy are inadequate. We are in charge. Political parties are replaceable, our country is not.

Politicians who betray the Constitution and our trust must be punished. Instead, we hear about numerous "investigations" that are spun and distorted with jumbled facts and shadowy people involved, leaving the media and the public confused. These investigations seem to be all for show value, to demonstrate that justice is indeed being served. After the investigation, a scapegoat or two is sacrificed on the altar of public opinion with home confinement, a short stint in club fed or a fine and it's back to business as usual. We have been told about numerous political scandals like Iran-Contra and Jack Abramoff, but what about the scandals that are never revealed? The probabilities are frightening.

This lack of trust in our government will test the strength of a country that must come to grips with a manageable position in world affairs. Our enormous commitments around the globe are a huge drain and unnecessary in the post-Cold War era. Instead of squandering resources abroad while our economy weakens and our citizens suffer for the sake of military-industrial interests, we must put our own house in order. We need to worry less about problems abroad and worry more about problems *in our own country*. Money spent on Iraq, Afghanistan and Haiti could be spent on New Orleans and our own aging infrastructure. We defend South Korea's border, but we can't defend our own borders. At present, it seems unlikely that our government will reduce its unwanted role as the world policeman. Certainly, our foreign policy changed forever after the horrid events of September 11, 2001. But those acts of terrorism could have been prevented with strong *internal* security measures. America is dealing with enemies in a multi-polar world that Cold War strategies can not defeat. Conservatives argue that America must be prepared for a new challenge from a "resurgent" Russia, a country that is no longer a legitimate threat to the United States or the NATO alliance.

Then there are the questionable claims and

fear mongering about the strength of Venezuela, Iran and moribund North Korea to justify massive military expenditure. Threats are easily magnified to beef up defense budgets. We were repeatedly told that Saddam Hussein was a threat with weapons of mass destruction. In the eyes of people around the world, it is the United States that is threatening.

The dangers are great when a nation devotes too much of its strength for military-industrial budgets, because government services that the taxpayers fund are diminished or eliminated for the world power role. The Soviet Union made that mistake, contributing to its destruction. We should all be proud of our brave men and women in the armed forces, but they should not be used as pawns to build an empire and they should never be placed in harms way for corporate interests.

Our nation must be strong at *home*. We need a prosperous economy that *all workers* can succeed in. Clearly, this is not the present reality, despite Wall Street rhetoric in the country. Too many Americans live from paycheck to paycheck, struggling with high rents, stagnant wages and debt.

People are tired of hearing empty political promises about improving our society and tired of corruption scandals and lies. Why should anyone pity CEOs, millionaires and billionaires who snivel for bailouts and more tax breaks? These people comprise a tiny minority who exploit us to live like royalty. Sympathize instead with the working poor, mothers struggling to raise children with low paying jobs, hardworking Americans losing their jobs because of offshoring and excessive immigration, the homeless, and for men and women in their twenties stuck in the family home because they can't afford their own, or the parents depend on their son/daughters income to help pay their own housing costs. These are all symptoms of an ailing economy. I'm not talking about people who have trouble coping with the realities of working for a living and I'm not talking about ex-convicts or people with drug and alcohol problems either. I am talking about millions of intelligent, talented and hardworking people who are going absolutely nowhere in this country. Stop throwing stones at your fellow citizens who suffer. The problem is not with the American people, the problem is a greedy system unchecked by business lobby government.

Sometimes, you have to stop questioning your own abilities and efforts. There are countless socio-economic circumstances beyond our control. Perhaps we should question instead, the anti-family/anti-worker tactics of the rich and our government. That is why I wrote American Dissident. As an American citizen, I have stopped my self-criticism and instead, I am questioning the abilities of our local, state and federal governments and the legitimacy of our rigid, corporate dominated economic system. This book does not reflect a strict liberal or conservative philosophy. These stale labels have divided Americans for decades. This book addresses the simple realities in America and with the irrefutable lessons of history, offers sensible, moderate solutions from the author with the input of working Americans to reinvigorate a society in decline.

Plutocracy

Monday 6:00 am: another workday begins in America. From Los Angeles to New York City, the same routines unfold as alarms go off and coffee pots are turned on to roust the workforce for another dose of the daily grind. It's always the same lame game. You get out of bed after *5-8* hours of sleep and stumble into the bathroom to clean yourself up. You shower, shave, brush your teeth, apply various cosmetics and put your clothes or uniform on. Then you turn on the television, computer or radio and inspect the refrigerator and cupboards for a quick breakfast. You ate pretty well over the weekend, but now the cupboards are rather bare and the refrigerator only contains leftovers and several ketchup, mayonnaise and salad dressing containers. That's when you get a little irritated and blame yourself or your partner for not buying more food with the last paycheck. But you're hungry now, so you're thinking about doing what millions of others do, stopping at a fast food restaurant on the way to work and consuming it during the commute. Of course, it's unhealthy to eat it, your cholesterol is over 200 and that once trim body is getting flabby in the wrong areas, but you can make another commitment to improving your eating habits when you have time. Your home is cluttered with dirty dishes and unfolded clothes and it seems like you just left the place, but you're headed for the door and on your way back to work.

So the workers hit the streets in cars, on foot or on bicycles to begin their commutes. For some, the city bus is the means of transportation and they rush to be at the bus stop on time or a few minutes early, because if they miss the 7:15, they'll be late and in trouble with the boss. They fumble around in their pockets and purses for their passes and coins. When the bus rumbles to the stop, the commuters climb aboard looking for their favorite seats, taking care to avoid drunkards and homeless types and watch their neighborhoods go by.

On the nations roadways, the mad dash to

work begins as commuters fight the traffic tooth and nail so they won't be late. Sometimes, a quick stop at a gas station is needed because you're on E. Honking horns and dead stops on the freeway are common occurrences in our cities, making the frustrating task of getting to work a job in itself. Unfortunately, you're not on the clock for this, even if you are spending time and money to get to and from work. Even though your city has been growing, additional roads and the widening of existing ones is done too slowly or never at all. Then people wonder why there are so many episodes of road rage. People wonder where the gas tax revenues went too. They're supposed to pay for these improvements.

Some drivers worry about getting pulled over for driving with burned out tail-lights that they don't have the time or money to fix.

Other commuters sweat every time they drive to work, or anywhere for that matter, because they're behind the wheel with suspended licenses and/or no auto insurance. They may owe child support or owe the state money for traffic tickets, but they still have to get to work to settle these debts. Some drivers worry about getting their vehicles started at all because they're ready for the junkyard. Those are the cars you poke fun at as you roll down the street, the 1980s and 90s vehicles with peeling paint, rust, cracked windshields, dents and too many bumper stickers. But no matter how you get to work and regardless of how expensive or dilapidated your vehicle is, you're in the same trap as everyone else. You are performing your role in the American rat race.

For many of us, it is a very unpleasant role because we know what's in store for us when we arrive at work. You have to answer to well connected people you do not respect. They expect respect, when it is earned, not given. Just because she's related to a department head or dating a "higher up" makes her better than you somehow. Just because he's a friend of the owner makes him qualified to be your manager. Then there are the days when you are worn out or frankly don't feel like going to work because of illness. Then there are the never ending childish games, superiors with their little titles and egos; lots of gossip, backstabbing and brown-nosing to "move up." It's really quite pathetic. There are so many things at home that need to get done, piles of bills and so little time for spouses and children. But now, it's back to the grindstone for more stress and monotony.

In the daily struggle for survival, American workers resort to desperate measures to meet consumption and rental/lease obligations. Millions are forced to take a second or third job, working 70 or 80 hours a week and it still isn't enough to "get ahead." There are only 24 hours in a day and 168 in a week, so if a worker spends 70 hours a week at work, that only leaves 98. Then there is the commute time (and gas money) spent going from job to job and job to home. Naturally, human beings have to sleep, so if you manage to get 7-8 hours each night, (a challenge in America) that's another 49-56 hours used each week for rest. So, depending on the length of the commutes, he/she would be fortunate to have 40 hours a *week* left over for family, errands, study, cooking, cleaning, exercise and leisure. (a life) That's a pretty tight schedule. No wonder foreign visitors claim that "All Americans do is work." Undoubtedly, time constraints like these (and low wages) pose enormous challenges to maintaining a marriage and raising children. In addition, it's downright stressful and stress kills.

Why are so many of us forced to work excessively long and hard to survive? It's really not rocket science. Low wages are the main culprit along with excessive taxation and crushing housing costs. But the government and the idle rich defend the status quo because they're quite happy and comfortable with the rules of this game, the very rules that keep them on top in their easy chairs and the workers below in the struggle. They have much to lose if the vast majority finally realize their plight and demand *real* economic and political reform. The elite remind us via Wall Street and Hollywood that their system works well and is a shining example for the world. With this cartoon capitalist realism, we're shown smiling people on television with big houses and fancy cars. We're spoon fed propaganda about how easy it is to start a business and live the "American Dream." According to people like John Stossel, the invisible hand of the free market will save us. Just take the advice of people like Jean Chatzky. If you're grateful and save your nickels and pennies, it's easy to get rich.

For the idle rich, it is easy. They can sleep in all day when they feel like it. They can call their secretaries and say that they won't be in the office because they have an important business meeting to attend. Then Mr. or Ms. Rich will hang up and roll in the sack with their lover or have another poolside drink brought to them at a snazzy resort.

Americans are told about a few "self made" success stories of individuals who were born into poverty or mediocrity, but with hard work and an unwavering desire to achieve financial freedom, the poor immigrant or entrepreneur became a wealthy American. Then this "successful person" will boast about the great risks they took and the tough times they endured, but they somehow rose above the misery and got a business started or made a key real estate deal. They got a lucky break and claim that opportunities are all around us. Supposedly, any American can do it. "I did it and so can you." How many times have we heard this before?

In fact, many wealthy Americans inherited their money. It's easy to score runs when you're born on second or third base. It's easy to start a business with daddy's 0% interest loans and business connections. Even when we go back to English colonization, blue blood families grabbed the lion's share of America's wealth. Enormous chunks of virgin land were handed over to a privileged few. They did not receive these lands for being exceptionally intelligent, innovative or hard working.

They were given these lands because they had personal connections with the royal family and powerful aristocrats. It's not what you know, but who you know. (and who you blow)

To make big money you have to squeeze it out of the earth or people. So, the prime cash crop growing regions were plundered for cotton, tobacco and wheat. Indentured servants were exploited throughout the colonies. Further expansion to the west at the expense of native Indians brought more wealth for a few from timber and furs. In the southern colonies, African slavery swelled the profits of plantation owners. In fact, it was the rich of Europe and the New World who were responsible for the slave trade. Solely for personal profit, they engaged in one of the largest human displacement and exploitation crimes of all time. It was the wealthy who financed the Trans-Atlantic voyages and made the dirty "free market" deals. This vicious cycle of favoritism, nepotism and exploitation that began with the colonization of the continent has continued to the present day, keeping the bulk of America's wealth in the hands of a select few. Despite demands for fairer economic opportunities and even redistributions of national wealth, the canyon between the "haves and have nots" remains and grows larger everyday.

Affirmative action is a halfhearted, misguided attempt to alter the condition. Millions of *working class* white males are paying the price for the centuries of slavery and discrimination that was not administered by indentured servants and others comprising the lower economic classes, but by the wealthy. It was the rich who were responsible for the discriminatory policies executed within their businesses, policies that were backed up with local, state and federal legislation by our past political leaders. They believed incorrectly that the free market would sort this all out, government would just get in the way. As usual, the working classes and the poor have to pay for the crimes committed by the rich, scapegoats for a cruel past. Racism itself is passed off as ignorance and hatred expressed predominantly by poor white males who are branded as "rednecks" or "hicks." The poor are blamed, but the blood is on the hands of the rich.

The rich of yesterday utilized African slavery, indentured servants and imported Chinese labor to do their dirty work and fatten their bottom lines.

The rich of today manipulate free trade and immigration policies. With the U.S. Chamber of Commerce acting on their behalf, they've whined for NAFTA, CAFTA, less union power, more temporary agencies, more productivity, more immigrants, more tax breaks and bailouts and all of their wishes have been granted. But they still can't compete. The hated overtime laws are in their sights. What will they want next? Their raging thirst for cheap labor and profit is never quenched. These vampires and their bribed politicians are simply unwilling to keep decent job opportunities right here in this country where they belong and would rather employ the rest of the planet instead of hard working people at home. As long as they're in cozy gated communities with fat profits and bonuses, they simply don't care about the condition of our country.

Now ask yourself, does this system work well for *you?* Or is the time right for cleaner capitalism? Have you ever been forced to pawn off valuable possessions just to pay the rent or buy food? Have you ever found yourself digging under couch cushions to find change for a lousy pack of cigarettes or bus fare? Take a good look at a plasma center and you will see people bleeding just to get a few dollars in their pockets until the next check arrives. Ask the homeless if this system works for them. Ask the man standing along a freeway exit ramp with a "Will work for food" sign. Ask adults living with their parents in their twenties and thirties. Ask the college graduates waiting tables and the elderly who survive on puny social security checks and reside in miserable nursing homes and closet sized apartments.

Instead of looking down on these people and assuming that they're lazy, stupid or incompetent, (as the system trains us to think) try to understand that no one plans or wants to live like this. Too many of us are wrecked by this system, far too many hopes and dreams perish because of it. In a society where nothing is free, lack of opportunity destroys.

Millions of us struggle with unemployment, underemployment, degrading temporary jobs and debt. Social critics are quick to blame our lack of interest in science and math, work ethic, unions, Generation X, lack of ambition and spending habits. Unfortunately, too many struggling people believe this pro-business fiction and Wall Street cheerleading and blame themselves instead of lack of opportunity. For these unfortunate ones, self-esteem is damaged as they sink lower in the class structure while others around them flaunt their cash and seemingly enjoy life to the fullest. Perhaps you've been there. Think of those frustrating, difficult times when expectations were not met and potential was stymied. I write with complete sincerity on this point because I have tasted poverty myself. I don't have a fancy Ivy League degree, but with nearly 25 years of experience, I have a Ph.D in working for a living. I understand what it's like to not eat properly, to lose your home and do without simple necessities like a car and decent clothing.

There are few punishments greater than being poor in a greedy society like ours. Poverty is a curse as months and years of your efforts crumble before your eyes; savings are lost, possessions are lost, friends are lost. Those are the difficult times when thorough job searches yield only miserable daily labor, part-time and temporary positions. Finally, you are forced to take these jobs far below your ability and standards because of complete desperation. Then you are worked like a mule and discarded like trash for virtually any reason. Degrading, hazardous and stressful jobs are assigned while the "real" employees look on.

Then the pathetic, little check is collected, which is already spent because of the debt accumulated from your rotten financial condition, hitherto borrowing money just to survive. You can find this suffering and exploitation at the many daily pay establishments across the nation. They're looking for "bodies" to perform the least desirable jobs in their communities.

The daily pay/temporary trap has ensnared millions of Americans. To get a taste of working reality, I urge Americans to take a hard look at the daily pay employers. I have, and I was disgusted by what I saw. Typically, you'll see lines of workers forming outside the daily pay joint at 5 or 5:30 am. They'll stand around smoking, coughing and spitting in the darkness hoping for a job. Around 6 am, the place opens for business and the assignments are given out. Some of the workers have "repeats" so they depart immediately. Some have to wait around until 7 or 8 am for a job. By 9 am, the jobs for the day are running out, but there will still be people waiting for their "daily bread." Some looked thin and sick. I saw people shaking from drug and alcohol withdrawl and smoking cigarette butts retrieved from trash cans.

This is America. This really happens. You will

find this in inner city neighborhoods plagued with high crime, barred windows, graffiti, feral dogs and cats and burned out buildings, but you will find this in the suburbs too. People like these (the working poor in general) rarely appear on any government statistic, because they have either exhausted unemployment benefits or simply do not qualify for them. Since they are "employed" they rarely qualify for any public assistance whatsoever. Then people wonder why millions of Americans stay on welfare or drop out of the job market completely.

Many of the people I met at daily pay joints abandoned their families because they could not provide child support. Some were drunks. But several were obviously intelligent and skilled. They had good jobs in the past, but when corporate downsizing and outsourcing took place, they were utterly destroyed. These are some of the workers "left behind" by free trade, NAFTA and out of control globalization. In a society run by an arrogant government and greedy, uncaring elite, nothing is done to help workers in these desperate situations. They are exploited for their cheap labor once by the company that uses their work and again by the daily pay joint that sells them like whores to the highest bidder. Seeing this cold reality for myself left an eternal impression on me. Citizens who work, pay taxes and contribute to our society should not be treated like this. But this is just one of many examples of a system that a few use to exploit the masses. The rich will utilize every dirty trick to increase their profits and nothing else matters to them, regardless of the suffering that is inflicted on the American worker and our country as a whole.

It is a system that demands constant sacrifice to keep your head above water. Year after year, we struggle to pay the bills and survive to the point when the unacceptable becomes acceptable. You see, a survival lifestyle is forced on you for so long that you actually grow accustomed to it. You get used to it. You settle for mediocrity and somehow get by or make "ends meet." When people complain or point out genuine statistics revealing that the U.S. economy is a wreck, we hear the old, tired rhetoric about how well off we are in America. We are reminded of starving and backward masses in other countries and told about the superiority of our economy. Never mind that many workers in the European Union, Japan, Australia and Canada live more comfortably than their American counterparts. According to pro-corporate authors, billionaires and their public relations teams, our standard of living from top to bottom is second to none.

It is a system of survival and this can be defined as being able to afford food, clothing and shelter. One may claim that the vast majority of our citizens do in fact enjoy these necessities, but there are homeless Americans in this land of opportunity. For the rest of us who have the three basics, I must ask what kinds of food, clothing and shelter we have? Soup and crackers? Fast food diets? Do you depend on food stamps? How about second hand clothing? Trailer parks and housing projects? Do you live in your car? Do you live in motels? Concerning nutrition, we're supposed to consume nutritional meals everyday that meet the U.S. recommended daily allowance (R.D.A.) of vital nutrients required for good health.

This is necessary to contribute to the development and preservation of a healthy mind and body. But in a nation with such an abundance of food, its malnutrition problems are often ignored. When you go shopping at the local supermarket or convenience store, you don't see any shortages. The shelves are crammed with any product you want. America produces and imports a lot of food and even though it takes such a big bite out of your finances, it is indeed a pleasure to load up that shopping cart. But beware of partially hydrogenated oils, hormones, artificial colors, sugars and sodium. These poisons are wrapped up in attractive packaging and marketed with slick advertising to fatten corporate bottom lines. They don't care about your health or the health of your children, they only care about sales. Yes, the shelves are crammed with food and for poor Americans this is another reminder of financial inadequacy as they carefully restrain what they spend. At least there are coupons, generic brands, bottom shelf and half price due to dating merchandise for them.

Millions of our children suffer at or below the "official" poverty line. Uncounted millions go to bed with growling stomachs every night. Uncounted millions more do not eat properly, due to skipping meals or consuming junk food. The fast food industry has cashed in on this reality by offering quick meals to overworked and underpaid Americans who do not have the money and/or time to prepare healthy, home cooked ones. But these realities are invisible to you as you wait in that long grocery line with your cart or basket of food; at least for three of four days anyway, that's how long it really lasts. When you find yourself taking the last slice of bread, what will you do until the next paycheck arrives? You will do what you usually do; skip meals, eat out of vending machines, use your credit card for small purchases, hit fast food joints, borrow money or simply starve.

Survival has a price. There is a price tag attached to everything we do, every action and every need; from the food you consume to the clothes you wear, to the roof over your head, to the bills you pay to keep the water running and the lights on. This cycle never ceases. You must have the money to pay for these necessities or you simply will not have them. If there is any interruption in your finances, you face the risk of eviction or going hungry. The rent is due every month, the utility bill is due on a monthly or bi-monthly basis and your body requires nourishment on a daily basis. Just because your cash flow is interrupted or diminished does not mean that your financial liabilities will wait for you to catch up.

You may have to borrow money to sustain yourself, which leads to debt peonage for the simplest necessities. When the rent is past due, the landlord doesn't want to hear excuses, he wants the money. There are no respites. Your stomach will not stop digesting while you look around for a job. When your car payment is past due and you can't come up with the dough, the bank doesn't want to hear promises, it wants the cash. Otherwise, you'll be dodging the repo man and eventually your car will be taken away. When the winter arrives and there's a chill in the air, you must have your utility bill paid to keep your home warm. If you can't pay it, you will shiver and suffer in the dark. During the summer, people are cooked alive in houses and apartments without air conditioning. But the utility company won't send flowers to the funeral, they just want the cash.

The water you drink and the air you breathe have a cost because of the taxes you pay to protect their quality. When you engage in sexual intercourse, there is a cost for the condom you use. In addition to the cost of a product or service, local, state and federal governments have their hands out for their cuts of your money. When a 30 year mortgage is finally paid off, the new owner rejoices! After paying off the outrageous loan, that crushing monthly payment is gone. The house is his right? Wrong. The home/property taxes must be paid for the rest of the "owners" life. If they are not, the city will take the house away. It never stops.

Our economic system is a combination of cutthroat capitalism and excessive taxation. The taxes we pay are supposed to fund social safety nets in case of bad fortune, boom and bust cycles inherent in capitalism itself. But when workers reluctantly turn to these programs for help, many are strangled by bureaucratic red tape, meeting determined resistance from state and federal government when requesting unemployment compensation, food stamps or welfare. They don't mind taking our tax dollars, but they sure don't like giving them back. Do we embrace this system because it's the only one that works or superior? Or do we accept it because we have no choice in the matter? The real question should be, is this system humane? This system was not bestowed to man by God with gospel truth principles, it is a man made one with many flaws and a brutal history that will be shown very clearly in this book.

Because of its weaknesses and inability to benefit anyone other than the idle rich and a small professional class, many Americans are deeply in debt and clinging to financial survival by their fingernails. The suffering is not obvious in most cases, we don't have famine outbreaks and plagues that kill millions. Instead, it's a condition of struggle and stagnation. An individual may live in a respectable neighborhood and wear decent clothes, but to sustain this vision of affluence, sacrifices must be made in other areas of his lifestyle. He has to rely on mass transit because the costs of a car and insurance coverage would *force* him to trim the rent, food and wardrobe budgets. Then there are people who can afford the cars, but can't afford to live in decent neighborhoods. Sacrifices like these are made because of stagnant wages and rising costs. Perhaps we could all buy new GM cars and trucks if we moved into slum neighborhoods and shopped at second hand stores.

Sometimes, workers encounter flash in the pan prosperity, a dead cat bounce. These are brief episodes of financial freedom after getting a tax refund, cashing out 401k savings or getting a new credit card. But they are the exception, not the rule. The drudgery of paycheck to paycheck survival swiftly returns and the party's over. But America is a rich country right? Everyone has lots of money here. This is the sham perception and anticipation of conditioned citizens. If you are not "successful" then you are weak, a loser, and bring dishonor to your family. This is especially true among people in their teens and twenties. Since they're too young and inexperienced with the *realities* of the working world, they emerge from high school or college with an inflated confidence of achieving success. They can easily get a six figure salary and retire when they're 35 or 40 right? They wonder why their parents and older siblings aren't more successful. But when he/she is struggling with the rent on an apartment because of the disappointing earnings of an entry-level job, they see more clearly through this fog of lies created by the elite. When they see co-workers repeatedly passed up for promotions and insulted with puny raises over the years, they grow up a little more. When they discover that people will have to die in order for them to move up the corporate ladder, they'll finally see for themselves the entrenched cycle of nepotism and favoritism that victimized their parents and prevented them from achieving their full potential. Now it's the kid's turn.

Neutron CEOs like Jack Welch, Wal-Mart

wages, temporary agencies, free trade fraud and a pro-corporate government can turn the optimistic financial dreams of our young people into nightmares.

Even though the vast majority of us struggle under the rule of the rich, we can not admit it. We must endure and appear content. Keep putting on your display of pseudo-sophistication, look professional, walk with confidence and don't complain about your debt, stress and poverty because it's your own fault. This learned hopelessness and passive compliance are the consequences of an abusive system used by a tiny privileged class to preserve their lofty positions and keep the rest of us under heel. It is an organized, determined effort by big business, the media and government to shape our views and defend a rigid caste system that rewards the comfortable and exploits the rest.

Wage Slavery

It is insulting to the American public to witness the enormous success of corporations, while the people who get the jobs done are treated like dirt by the owners and management. The founder's idea is nothing without the infrastructure and hard work to make his dream a reality. But the hard work is rarely appreciated because it's *expected* and he always wants more. We even hear stories about the company not making any money or silent partners to compensate. The owner is broke. The rich and their top managers use stories like these to deny wage increases and improved benefits to their employees. To keep costs down and "compete" the business won't cough up any raises despite increased productivity. Put simply, the owner wants more out of you, but he doesn't want to pay for it. He wants a free lunch.

The reverse psychology job is used to the point where a worker will feel sorry for the owner. Yes, a struggling wage slave pitying a snobbish multi-millionaire.

Meanwhile, he's expanding, not only in the United States, but on a global scale. The profits are fat and sweet, but they're only going into the pockets of a select few. An excellent example of this swindling is in the American restaurant/ hospitality industry. Hotel and fast food chains claim to have thin profit margins and this is used as one excuse to pay minimum wages while providing minimal benefits or none at all. But these places are everywhere, some of these chains possess thousands of stores. Unfortunately, the bulk of the people who make your reservations and serve your food are treated contemptuously by the public and poorly paid. The hospitality industry refuses to pay a 21st century American wage and hounds our government for more immigrants instead.

Restaurant and hotel chains are goldmines, but the CEO will talk to employees about corporate debt, depreciation, taxes, interest on corporate debt and a lot of other made up and exaggerated shit to downplay the real success of the company. He will say this with a straight face after he cashed his mega-million dollar bonus check. The company's stock value increases, so the fat rats at the New York Stock Exchange cash in as well. But what about the people who really did the work? Once again, they are told a pack of lies about the company losing money or breaking even, so they must work harder and smarter! Of course, the reverse psychology jobs and lies are not limited to the hospitality industry. Under globalization and raw capitalism, this is the way of doing business in every industry of the American Plutocracy.

The demolition of worker rights for the sake of lobbyists and corporate power is ongoing and sinister. Hard earned labor rights have been swept aside and the bad old days are back for the American worker. The elite have done this by shoving the government and unions out of the labor rights formula, leaving wage earners at the mercy of big business.

The temporary worker tactic is in full swing, giving workers second class status and no benefits, swelling the ranks of Americans without health insurance. The corporations argue that they require temporary workers "to compete" and meet labor shortages on a short term basis since they can't afford to hire them. However, they don't have a problem with keeping workers temporary on a permanent basis; that is, as a "permatemp" to get the same job done that the company's direct hires are doing for a fraction of the cost. This degrading form of exploitation (similar to indentured servitude) is increasing as the temp agencies fatten from the blood sucked out of the American worker. It's bad enough to be exploited by one company, but when you're a temp, you're exploited by two. Both profit immensely from the temps work, but the agency is an unnecessary middleman between you and the job.

The agency scours help wanted ads on the Internet and in local newspapers and offers to fill positions at a lower cost than a company would have paid had it hired the worker on its own. Along with illegal immigration and outsourcing, the temporary agencies apply downward pressure on American wages. For example, a warehouse places an ad seeking two experienced forklift operators. The warehouse is willing to pay $12-14 an hour DOE with medical and 401k benefits. But like a hungry hyena, a salesperson from the agency will zero in on the ad and offer two fork-lift operators for $17 an hour each. This is a bargain for the warehouse because $17 an hour is *all they'll pay.* Legally, these operators will work for the agency, so the warehouse is relieved of insurance and tax obligations for them. They can also be disposed of for whatever reason at any time, so it's a cheap and easy arrangement for the warehouse.

Now, the agency sends two operators and pays them $10.50 *an hour with no benefits.* A job that once promised $12-14 an hour with benefits has suddenly become a $10.50 an hour job with none. The warehouse wins with cheaper labor and less paperwork, the agency wins by making a tidy profit from the warehouse and the agency salesperson gets a fat bonus. So everyone wins... except the two operators...People call the warehouse or send their resumes for the job openings, but it's too late. The jobs are gone, snatched up by the temp agency.

Temps are used to do undesirable work and absorb insults from permanent employees behaving like supervisors despite lacking the title. Temps are used so permanent workers can take their vacations and breaks at a time of their choosing and used as convenient scapegoats for production and office errors.

One may argue that it is better to be at the mercy of big business (the idle rich and their handpicked management) than to be at the mercy of big government. But in America, the people are supposed to be in control, the people are supposed to govern. So why should we be slaves to either? We must restore the balance between big business and labor. If the politicians really executed the will of the people (if they did their jobs) and were not in the pockets of the rich and lobbyists, then this fair balance could be achieved. Our citizens would work under fair regulations with good pay and benefits and temporary employment and offshoring would be curtailed. Government and unions would make certain that these conditions were realities in all 50 states, not empty promises or loop holed legislation supposedly requiring them, but reality.

Our government is our best defense (along with unions) against greedy businesses. It must act on behalf of working people, not corporate lobbyists. Government has a role; not to strangle the business with bureaucratic red tape and frivolous lawsuits, but to ensure good pay for jobs well done in a safe working environment.

When corporations abuse the environment and people in the community they do business in, they must be punished. Unfortunately, they rarely are. The cases get tied up in the courts for years, even decades. Exxon is a prime example. The 1989 Exxon Valdez oil spill is among America's worst environmental disasters. The company appealed punitive and compensatory damages all the way to the Supreme Court. The 19 years of stall tactics worked; the company got a slap on the wrist, a wink to big business that they can get off easy.

When a company gets in hot water with federal, state or local government on environmental, labor or tax laws, top management will cry the blues about being unable to reduce emissions or pay the fines. The company will remind the regulatory agency and the public that they employ people in the community and it would be wise to back off or go easy on it to keep people on the job. Otherwise, the company will threaten to layoff employees, outsource jobs or leave the area completely and setup shop in Mexico or China.

Local politicians need to keep unemployment down in their districts or towns, so they don't want a business layoff or outsource because of sanctions they apply on it. The business will blame the government for the pink slips even though the business brought the penalty upon itself by breaking laws. In addition, the businesses lobby legislators to dilute the budgets and vigor of regulatory agencies, resulting in lax or nonexistent enforcement. When businesses are left to regulate themselves and government is in bed with the companies, consumers are threatened. Consequently, Americans have been killed and hospitalized due to frequent salmonella and E. coli outbreaks. Why should anyone die from eating a hamburger or peanut butter sandwich? Why should anyone worry about drinking tap water or breathing the air outside? This has to change, the government and its regulatory agencies must consistently enforce their own laws. They must show some backbone and stand up to corporate criminals. When firmer regulation is discussed, the rich whine about "big government" and "socialism." Keeping government at bay and workers under heel is the name of the game.

Despite the rhetoric about corporations and multi-billionaires donating to charity, they really don't care about their own workers or poor

Americans. Their cutthroat tactics have swelled the ranks of people dependent on charity here. Throwing pocket change and used clothing their way will not cure the damage. Building schools in Africa and adopting children in Asia does nothing for America. Laying workers off here and donating abroad hurts our country. They donate to enhance the reputation of the business, for publicity stunts and above all, for tax write offs. All they care about is their bottom lines and donating can fatten them.

Even when profits grow continually, top management will find more "innovative" ways to squeeze every dime they can get out of their workforce. When productivity has reached an all time high and orders are rolling out ahead of schedule, they will repress the smiles and chastise the workers, claiming that productivity slipped and the orders are behind schedule. The owners use their top managers to announce sham statistics and enforce measures to bring the business in line with his greedy, unrealistic goals. The managers apply sneaky, manipulating tactics to suck your blood (labor and ideas) until you're dry to get their bonuses and look good before the owner that pulls his/her strings. The "performance goals" which are really commands, are announced and those who fall short of achieving them will be ridiculed or fired.

If you dare to question or challenge a bellicose manager, you can be "set up" for termination. The challenge may simply be a request to modify scheduling or a production scheme. No one knows your job better than you, even if your bosses' boss thinks he does. You may present a simpler or superior way of getting the job done. If the idea is implemented, the manager will take credit for using his people well or claim that the idea was his from the start. An employee with clever ideas may be viewed as an internal threat by the manager and it is wise to be on guard when sharing your expertise in a company that views you as a disposable pack animal or cog. The set up can be just about any petty violation of company procedures. When on good or neutral terms with management, these "violations" are ignored. But when you're in the doghouse with management, these violations suddenly become very serious business.

Being a few minutes late for work, declining a request to work overtime or forgetting to sign a checklist that is seldom signed anyway are now considered insubordination or sub-standard performance. In other words, the owner or manager doesn't like you and he/she is in the process of getting rid of you. Thus, merit has no importance in a scenario like this. What matters is whether the manager likes you (politics) or has a continuing use for you. He/she merely needs an excuse to terminate you to diminish the possibility of a lawsuit and deprive you of unemployment benefits.

When an employee asks for a raise, it's like asking for a night with the owner's wife. The response is often "we can't afford any raises" or management will find an insignificant flaw in the worker's job performance and use it as an excuse to deny the request. They seem to think that we'll work for anything or be satisfied with the same wage we were making 5 years ago. We're working there for the fun of it right? Often, raise requests are simply ignored or a how dare you ask attitude is displayed. This disgraceful behavior is all too common in the workplace. Prices rise, but the paychecks rarely follow suit. The rich get richer, the poor get poorer and the workers stagnate.

Since the paychecks have not kept pace with prices and inflation, many working people have reluctantly turned to credit cards and loans to supplement their dwindling net incomes. Increasing tax burdens have exacerbated this squeezing action, leaving millions one paycheck away from poverty. Yet, so much is expected from the worker and little or no reward comes along with the increased productivity and super job performance. With the increased production comes larger profits for the elite, bigger bonus checks for the upper middle and more tax revenues for the government. But instead of receiving higher wages and better benefits for their efforts, the antithesis has occurred. The paychecks are stagnant or shrinking and the benefits (if any apply) require more employee compensation. Is this the American way?

Sure, the owner is entitled to his cut, legally it's his business, but what is it without a workforce? It is an empty structure where nothing gets done. No work=no profit=no tax revenues.

It really is that simple. Despite the pompous claims by entrepreneurs and CEOs that they "built this business" let us not forget that the owner rarely or never designs, manufactures, packs or ships the product. These critical stages are performed by workers, not the founder, who may be absolutely clueless about operating robots, repairing forklifts, driving 18 wheel rigs, balancing the books or creating a marketing mix. So what happened to the idea of making an *honest* profit and having a well paid workforce? That should be the American way, but instead, the owners and CEOs want to pursue a course of lavish extremes. They think they're entitled to do this even when the company performs poorly under their leadership. They want to play God and "live it up" like overpaid athletes and billionaires. While workers struggle to eat three decent meals a day and pay the rent, the rich enjoy morning massages, personal trainers, gaudy artwork, hearty meals prepared and served by their personal staff, satin sheets laundered daily by their maids, front row seats for sporting events, private jets, travel the world to chase solar eclipses, bodyguards, diamond rings for every finger of their lover's hands and groomed pets that eat more nutritious food than working families. Rex can feast on steak while workers nibble on hot dogs, instant soup and macaroni and cheese. We're told that life is tough and stressful for the rich. It's not true at all. They are coddled, soft and lazy.

Instead of reinvesting the bulk of the profit back into the business for new equipment and raises, the owner squanders it on fantasies and debauchery. When the fruits of the company's success are divided, much of the wealth goes to the owner's travel expenses, (tax deductible) corporate parties, outrageous management bonuses and advertising. The company can afford to dish out millions on Super Bowl commercials and company cars, but can not grant a loyal employee's request for a modest raise.

You know who the top managers are, the cocky group with the smelly perfumes/colognes and phony smiles, the people who get longer lunch breaks and are too good to eat with the "little people." At one time, some of them were general employees too, now they're too good to socialize with you. All too often, we see unqualified, lazy people in these positions. They climb the ladder by kissing up to the owner, sleeping with superiors and squealing on fellow employees. They often have a personal link to the owner or upper management, such as being a relative or friend of either. Sometimes, you'll see people get hired right off the street and installed as your manager because he/she went to the same college as your human resource manager or other "big shot."

It's a shame to see hard working, loyal employees who truly deserve management and supervi-
sory positions constantly passed up by parasites.
This scenario shows the workplace environment
at its worst. How can anyone expect a company
to excel and meet new challenges when you have
inexperienced and incompetent people making
key decisions? Instead of pursuing long-term
planning and solutions, like investing in their
own workforce, more efficient technology and
new plants, a short-term fix for quick profit has
been the focus of corporate executives. Group
think is not innovation; slashing wages, choosing
quantity over quality, outsourcing and downsizing are the consequences of their narrow-minded
policies.

The rampant cycle of nepotism and favoritism
in the workplace creates a hostile, cynical mood
among employees. If you criticize the hiring/pro-
motional system, the gossip will start and you'll
be labeled as a whiner. Once this reaches upper
management, they'll take you aside and explain
that if you're not happy with the company, then
"you know where the door is." They get so de-
fensive when someone dares to question a failing system. If you continue to "make waves" then

management can stir up trouble for you and find any excuse to terminate your employment. If you threaten to quit, they never seem too concerned. After all, they have the shallow attitude that all employees are replaceable and the position can be refilled by someone for a cheaper wage.

So you have to play by their rules and dance to their tune or you'll be out of a job. You need it to keep your life together, to keep your home and car. You have to tolerate this crap to keep the paychecks coming. If they stop, your life can swiftly fall apart. This is the power that the employer has over the employee. It is a power that employers understand all too well. You are an expendable "human resource" and by the owner's good graces, you are employed.

Many Americans have experienced the loss of a job, either by layoff or termination. It can be a devastating blow to your lifestyle and confidence. Relationships that were created with co-workers are destroyed since you're "no longer part of the team." All of your work and ideas are taken and then you're dismissed. I've seen men and women experience the pain of losing their jobs, usually for flimsy excuses like being a few minutes late once or twice within a 30 day period, common acts of carelessness that result in insignificant loss, inability to work overtime, or expressing opinions about the company or its management.

When I started a job as a receiving clerk in Orlando, Florida, one of my co-workers was a young woman who had put in 3 years of loyal service as a printing inspector. After my 90 day "probationary period" had elapsed, I was officially hired and I made a higher wage than she. Undoubtedly, she deserved more money, but the company used her attendance as an excuse to deny her requests for wage increases. She called in once or twice a month because she suffered from occasional migraine spells. She suspected the use of ammonia in the printing presses and poor ventilation as contributing factors to the headaches. But her performance was solid and the printing pressmen rarely slipped a defective label past her piercing brown eyes. She was well liked by her co-workers, not only in her quality control department, but throughout the plant. She did not make a lot of money, only $300-$350 net weekly paychecks, but she financed a car and was always well dressed and groomed for work with new jeans and shirts. She *appeared* to be comfortable financially.

In April, she took her vacation and used the time to move from Orlando to Daytona Beach, about 40 miles northeast of the plant into a studio apartment facing the ocean blue. This may have overextended her commute a bit, but her car was dependable and if the traffic wasn't too bad, she could drive to work in 40-50 minutes and return home in roughly the same amount of time. The woman was improving her lifestyle in many ways and when she returned from vacation, she seemed happy and proud of her achievements. In early May, the migraines started again and she called out. It was nothing new, everyone knew what was going on, she would be back tomorrow. On May 8, she was back and it seemed like another ordinary day on the job for her and everyone else for that matter. But it wasn't. She was walking toward the employee exit, saying a few words to the pressmen as she made her way to the door. I walked up to her and heard the words "they let me go" to the last pressman on the production line. When I stopped in front of her, I asked what was going on and her eyes met mine. I will never forget that look on her face, a face trying to look cool and emotionless, but her eyes deceived the attempt. I could see the shock and sadness within them. "bye" she said. I was nearly speechless, but I managed to say "goodbye" before she left the building. The encounter lasted only 3 or 4 seconds, but it told a story. She was devastated and on the verge of tears. It was over, three years of work finished. Now a 5 year car loan and a new apartment to pay for and no job. This can happen to anyone at any time in America. No one is safe.

"We must compete!" It is the cry of corporate America and for the sake of being competitive, it is justifiable for executives to eliminate thousands of jobs to make the company leaner, to thin the herd. Justifiable to freeze wages and command employees to contribute more for medical benefits. Justifiable to move manufacturing to foreign lands, selling out their own country by robbing America of opportunities. American unions try to fight back, but they are outmaneuvered by management sending our jobs to Mexico and Asia where they are done for less pay and executed under lax or non-existent labor regulations. The company can take advantage of weak environmental laws in foreign countries and use them as dumping grounds for their industrial, chemical and pharmaceutical wastes. Foreigners are employed and the products are assembled for peanuts, then sold in America for handsome profits. These are the realities of free trade and Business Roundtable domination of our economy.

In America, good jobs are phased out to make way for cheap temporary employees. Union strength continues to wane in the 21st century as family wage jobs are being eliminated by export and replaced with pitiful service and low skill jobs that pay starvation wages with no benefits and no future. The smaller unions are virtually helpless to resist these trends to the point where they must merge with other unions to survive. Now a union only in name, still collecting the dues, but too weak to provide any progress and protection for its workers. This assault led by the idle rich and the government they control is nothing less than an attack on America's families and with sinister cunning and cutthroat tactics, they have wrecked the middle class and reduced millions of Americans to debt peonage and poverty.

Wall Street does not believe that economic success is measured by a strong middle class and decent living standards, it judges success by gross economic weight (GNP) and how many new millionaires and billionaires live in the country. With this twisted philosophy, their ultimate goals will make America a rich or poor society with a pro-corporate government, a tiny, super wealthy elite and plenty of "competitive" underpaid and over-taxed citizens to exploit. This crushing weight is destroying the future of our working people. To compete, the elite have transformed our society. We are expected to work very hard, pay heavy taxes and be content with low wages for our efforts. If we refuse, the floodgates are opened to more immigrants and they'll work for the wages we can't afford to work for.

The wages are bad enough as it is. Consequently, many Americans have to do without necessities like cars and decent housing. Some of us are *forced* to share our homes with others to pay the rent. Ask yourself if anyone can live comfortably making 25-30k a year. Most of the "new jobs" that the government talks about provide this or less. $10-13 an hour isn't going to cut it here in the 21st century after the government (at all levels) takes its tribute. Could you afford a decent apartment and eat 3 square meals a day on that? Could you afford a car, its gasoline, insurance coverage and maintenance? Could you save anything?

How about a trip to the dentist? How about a

phone, utility bills, credit card payments, haircuts and clothes? Or would you be forced to work a second job and/or look for a roommate to share your expenses? Think about it.

This is the drab reality that the rich and our government have created. If you want children on these wages, it can lead to misery for the family or single parent. The costs of child rearing can easily break the slim budgets of the American worker. Apparently our government believes that having babies is a privilege (like driving or having a decent job) and with more anti-worker and anti-family economics, they have imposed a very effective birth control on our citizens. Malthus would be impressed with their measures.

How many American women would stay home and raise children if her husband's income provided a comfortable lifestyle? Before the 1980s and Reaganomics, one income was sufficient for many American families. But those days are long gone and mothers and children have been damaged in the name of the free market. If one income provided a family wage and benefits again, American (not just immigrant) fertility rates would surely rise and the elite would have no excuse to import labor. "Labor shortages" that our government and corporations whine about would not exist. But we can't start and sustain a family with American expenses on Mexican wages. We're being rubbed out and replaced with Third World hordes.

When a man and a woman decide to start a family, one full-time income must provide the basic essentials such as food, housing, clothing, transportation and home furnishings. The parents should be able to purchase their child a crib, toys and learning aids to prepare him/her for the coming social/educational stages. There must be adequate time to spend with their son or daughter to teach responsibility and to instill discipline if necessary. These basic measures should be automatic for child rearing, the absolute minimum for any young human being to begin their journey on the road of life. But again, for financial reasons, our young citizens are delaying parenthood or planning not to have children at all.

This is truly a sad situation in the country and the economy is largely to blame for it. Big business and the government have made the decision for us. When both parents have *to work* just to sustain a minimal living standard, the child suffers by losing significant time with them. The child will not develop properly without the full-time attention of at least one parent. Instead, he will spend time at daycare or with a babysitter. Perhaps the child will be left alone completely, since many working parents can not afford daycare costs at all. Our wages continue to stagnate or decline and costs continue to rise. We spend more and more time at work and our paychecks get smaller and smaller in their relative buying power. The system controls everything we do through money and with a declining standard of living, (the race to the bottom) it has prevented many of us from having families and has prevented others from providing the basic comforts that all American children should enjoy. Diabolical, but true. According to a report by the USDA's Center for Nutrition Policy and Promotion, a middle-income family with a child born in 2008 will spend about $221,000 raising that child through age 17.

Of course, the rich have plenty of time and money for their children and their fortunes will be handed down to them. But for working people, the situation is all too common. They raise their children in cramped apartments and crummy houses in neighborhoods plagued with high crime and neglected schools. They must consume cheap, unhealthy food and rely on second-hand furnishings and clothing, which can damage the self-esteem of the child when he attends school in old, out of style clothes while a few of his classmates wear the newest fashions.

This is where the trap begins. This is where the class divisions appear. The working class children are often cursed with low self-esteem and poor living standards, while rich and professional class children enjoy the comforts of the system. The system needs plenty of future wage slaves for construction and office help, plenty of servants to serve and stiffs to clean. But it only requires a few to hold the high status jobs and even fewer to inherit the businesses. The system is a pyramid and to sustain it, this machine can not allow too many to climb to the upper levels. We must understand that the overwhelming majority of us are born to be wage slaves and it is nearly impossible to escape this fate. As usual, the rich and the government deny this and we are told that the American Dream is alive and well. But we know better.

Owning a home is indeed a dream, that is, an unrealizable one for many of us. Even the basics like reliable cars and new home furnishings are very difficult to obtain. Too many workers who drive must rely on old, tired cars or go up to their necks in debt by taking out loans (at loan shark rates) for a decent vehicle. If you depend on a "beater" to carry out life's demands, you can be harassed, jailed or fined by local and state police because the government actually profits from this form of poverty, from the inability of workers to pay for insurance coverage and general repairs. It's becoming a crime for workers and the poor to drive a car. Driving is a convenience like a washing machine or telephone that should be enjoyed by all responsible working people. But with stagnant wages and rising costs, this is yet another attempt to diminish our living standards and *freedom*. It looks like the government won't be happy until we're all on buses and bicycles.

Our government boasts about our nation's great wealth and the rich express their utmost confidence in the system. America, supposedly the richest nation on earth, appears to be so, at least from the outside looking in. But the myth is exposed once one examines the real economic situation in the country. Since savings rates are essentially zero, many Americans are one paycheck away from poverty. The government expects people to raise families on $25,000 annual

incomes or less. This is a level fit for the Third World, not the United States. When children are raised in such dire conditions, how can anyone expect them to become enlightened adults to carry the nation into the future? Is it any wonder why so many young adults are in prison or involved with gangs? They turn to gangs and crime because there are no employment opportunities. Jobs they could be working have been shipped off to other countries creating the "Rust Belt" and long unemployment lines from coast to coast. So what do we expect them to do? People have to eat and pay the rent. It's a bit hard to do so when there are no jobs, or the only available ones are part-time positions paying minimum wage. Then there are the superfluous degree demands by employers, illegals stealing jobs and job sites that can not be reached without a car. America's young people are especially hard hit by our weak job market and greed.

Those in the demographics dubbed "Generation X and Y" have experienced decline in their economic fortunes. Then parents wonder why their kids can't move out of the family home and stay *out*. The answer is very simple. The economy is too weak to meet the basic needs of its young citizens. So the young person languishes in the family home, unable to stand on his own financially, which retards his maturity, confidence and strength and he remains as a consequence, a child. His financial problems become the rest of the family's problems and the young person is blamed. The "Xers" in particular were shortchanged by a system that offered them little hope of achieving the relative prosperity of their parents. While many boomers enjoyed substantial gains during the Clinton era, Generation Xers lost ground and gave up on the American Dream. Instead of pointing the finger of blame at the government, the idle rich and the boomers themselves, it was pointed at the Generation Xers, who were branded as "slackers" and "whiners." The architects of out of control globalization, excessive immigration, outsourcing, union busting and free trade fraud were really to blame. These are all corporate schemes rubber-stamped by our pro-business government. The Xers financial future was sacrificed for the elite. Less pay for the Xers meant more pay for them, more bonuses and better bottom lines. If anyone wants to talk about class warfare, look no further. When the rich attack the working classes, it's healthy capitalism, but when working people try to defend themselves, it's socialism.

Getting out of mom and dad's house (or apartment) is a challenge for young, working people in this age of skyrocketing rents and flat wages. If you find a decent apartment or house, the monthly rent is a crushing expense that leaves little leftover for food and transportation. If you're fortunate enough to find a unit that won't break the bank, its condition is often deplorable, located in crowded, high crime areas.

In addition, cheap apartments and boarding house rooms are often tiny 1 or 2 room structures. (efficiency units and studios) Many boarding house units do not have private bathrooms, so 10 or 15 tenants must share 2 or 3 communal bathrooms. This can cause anxiety when nature calls unexpectedly or you're late for work and all of the bathrooms are occupied. Sanitation is an obvious concern and sandals must be worn when showering or treading on the floors.

If you're fortunate, your boarding room will have an oven and a refrigerator. If not, you'll be shopping from meal to meal, unable to cook and store perishable food. Air conditioning may not be available or it's a unit that should have been replaced decades ago. This can cause great suffering and even dehydration and death during the summer months. Affordable boarding houses, apartments, mobile homes and trailers are frequently infested with termites, ants, spiders, cockroaches, rats and other unwelcome pests because of cheap "slum lords" and incompetent management, exacerbating miserable living conditions. Despite the gardens, trimmed lawns and welcome mats, millions of Americans are living in places that were only reluctantly moved into because of financial realities. They can make some inexpensive cosmetic improvements, but a dump is a dump.

I'm writing about deplorable housing from personal experience. During my time in Orlando, Florida, I saw neighborhoods that resembled the dwellings of Third World nations, not a so-called First World one like America. The canyon between the "haves and have nots" is obvious throughout the Sunshine State in appalling ways despite state and local efforts to conceal its shabby neighborhoods from the eyes of tourists. I reluctantly moved into a trailer park community in northern Orlando. I was new to the state and my low paying maintenance job and lack of transportation limited my housing options. I had to room up with someone and be close to work. Scattered around my new home were approximately 20 trailers, forming a horseshoe alignment with three others in the middle. For $75 a week, I obtained a room about the size of an average bathroom, "furnished" with a battered chest of drawers and a crude twin sized bed. The full rent was $600 a month. I was paying half, while the woman who leased the trailer along with her son, paid the other half. It really wouldn't be fair to charge the $600 sum for a year. The unit, like the others around it, was infested with cockroaches and had constant plumbing problems that the manager promised to fix on several occasions with no results. Some of the trailers were inhabited by seniors, others by young families. One in particular was home for 8 residents. Even though their trailer had only 2 bedrooms, all of them were somehow packed inside as they did their best to disguise the over-crowding from the manager.

Wild grass and weeds grew all around the trailers and beer cans and bottles were strewn about. There were trees all around the park, but the shade provided little relief during the 85-90 degree afternoon heat. There was no air condi-tioning and fans did little to relieve the sweating and discomfort. Getting sleep was difficult. I tossed and turned because of the sticky, humid nights, buzzing mosquitoes and the racket from groups of people drinking beer outside. Finally, after 2 months of this misery, I found a second job and scraped up enough cash to move into an apartment 2 miles away. During my last week in the trailer park, an underground septic tank burst three units down from mine, enveloping the entire park in a nauseating stench of feces and urine. At the spot of the break, the sandy, weed covered ground dampened and to my disgust, children with no shoes and socks were playing in it with beach balls, toy trucks and dolls. The parents were nowhere in sight.

Trailer and mobile home parks are common throughout Florida and much of the southern United States and many of them are in awful shape. The general poverty in these parks has earned the residents degrading and humiliating classifications. They're often referred to as "white trash" or "trailer trash." But fixed incomes and the low wages in a "right to work state" like Florida keep the slum lords in business.

I met many people who were also new arrivals to the state. Some had visited Orlando, Miami or Daytona Beach while on vacation and they were dazzled by the warm weather, crowded beaches with scantily clothed, tan bodies and Disney theme parks. They returned to New York, Michigan, Ohio and several other northern states with the intention of returning to Florida on a permanent basis. But I heard many complaints about the low wages and many people who move to Florida ultimately return home because of that.

It was time for me to leave too. I had been planning a move to New Jersey for months. I couldn't take all of my worldly possessions with me on an airliner, so I packed only the absolute necessities; my best clothes, photographs, and a briefcase that contained a rough draft of the book you are reading now. My bed and other furnishings were reluctantly sold off or thrown away. I packed all I could into a couple of cardboard boxes, a carry on suitcase and a red duffel bag. A taxi pulled up on a sunny, Thursday morning and the destination was Orlando International Airport.

As the cab rolled down highway 436, I reflected on the 3 years I lived there, how it could have been better, what I could have done differently. There were good times and bad of course, but one bit of advice from a co-worker summed it all up.

"To make it here, you need 2 jobs or a real job."

"What city are you flying to?" asked the cab driver as he peered at me in the rear viewing mirror with squinted eyes. The daydream was interrupted. "Newark, New Jersey. I'm not coming back here, this is a permanent move." I said with a grin. "How long did you live here?" he asked. "Three years, that's enough time for this place." I said. "I've been here all my life.

If I had the cash, I would have been gone years ago, but I have bills and child support." he said as he changed lanes. "Florida is a tough place to live in, you have to make the bucks up north, then you can retire down here with the lower cost of living." the cabbie added. He was quite accurate with his analysis. Florida attracts millions of tourists and northern retirees. They arrive with their pensions, social security checks and cash from the sales of expensive homes. They can sell their houses in Massachusetts or New York for $500,000 or more and purchase one for half the price in Florida. But in a right to work state like Florida, the Floridians themselves have virtually no chance of buying the same houses. Along the coast from West Palm Beach to Miami, the rich long ago collectively inflated real estate prices far beyond Florida incomes. Sure, there are ritzy hotels, beachfront mansions and luxury cars, but most of these spoils are enjoyed by tourists and retirees from other states and countries.

At least there are theme parks for working Floridians, the giant cartoon lands for people to temporarily escape the general poverty and lethargy of their daily lives. But the prices are outrageous, not only for the entry passes, but for food, drinks and souvenirs. The theme parks are goldmines but the workers are miserably paid. The Floridians staff the hotels, guard the beaches and pools and serve in the restaurants and souvenir shops. They protect, serve and clean up after the tourists when they're done with their vacations. The northern retirees dominate the state with their financial and political influence from Tallahassee to Key West. Florida is really not for Floridians, but for invaders. "It's real simple." said the cabbie with an unlit cigarette hanging from his mouth. "It's a big stinkin' slave state."

So I moved to New Jersey and lived there for 2 years. The wages are higher in the northeast than in the south, but so are the taxes. Instead of trailer parks, there are low-income projects and very tough neighborhoods. Despite the hype about a "Newark renaissance" the city is still scary to visitors and commuters. "Cleaning up" a city is more complicated than building parks and tearing down public housing.

New York City has its Manhattan tourist traps and ritzy condos, but this is just a tiny slice of the Big Apple. Jimmy Carter called the South Bronx the worst neighborhood in America, but there are many more that look just like it, particularly in Brooklyn and the Bronx. If you have been to Bedford-Stuyvesant, (the do or die Sty) Coney Island, Flatbush, East New York, Morrisania or Tremont, you'll have a better understanding of America's greatest city than a politician or some movie star in a high rise with Central Park views. These neighborhoods need help. The money squandered on rebuilding foreign countries should be spent here.

I always wondered what the city government was doing as I walked by condemned warehouses, graffiti, burned out cars, abandoned shopping carts and littered streets. I saw the same mattresses and piles of garbage sitting in alleys for weeks among collapsing buildings fenced off years ago and left to rot. If the mayor doesn't care, why should anyone else?

Blue Collar/White Collar

We're always told about the necessity of a college education if you want a good job in America and the nation's employers require this from job applicants on an ever increasing scale. America's colleges and their sales and marketing teams have done an outstanding job of convincing Americans that their future is hopeless without a degree. Many companies will not even consider an individuals resume unless he/she has a 4 year degree. Anything less and it's automatically destined for the shredder. The degree demand has increased because American companies are cheap on training. They expect people to walk through the front door and perform the job at a superb level. Public school teachers (and their unions) are blamed for not preparing our young people for the "global economy."

Many Americans finish high school with excellent grades, but they're expected to go to work and move out of the family home soon after graduation. Some finish high school and consider college, but the costs are far beyond their means. There are also self-taught Americans and people who have had enough of thugs and drugs in classrooms when high school is finished or not.

Employment can not be denied on the basis of race, sex, color, national origin, religion, sexual orientation, veteran status or age in America. With so much legal emphasis on providing "equal employment opportunity" isn't this *automatic* disregard for non-college graduate workers really a practice of discrimination? It is a false, ignorant belief that a college degree applicant is always superior to one that is not, that a high school diploma is simply inadequate for today's "high tech jobs."

A degree will not tell you if the applicant is mature, honest, dependable, hard working, loyal, tough, sociable or drug free. A fool is a fool, with or without a degree. It's one thing to study a science or skill on a screen or chalkboard, but quite another to actually perform it. There is simply no substitute for on the job training and experience.

Many aging top managers attended college in the 1970s and 80s when the business world was quite different from what it is now. Primitive computers were seldom or never used, the Cold War was on, globalization was on hold and NAFTA did not exist. In many ways, the degrees earned then are obsolete. Yet, top managers expect applicants to have the "21st century skills" they often lack themselves.

There are plenty of jobs out there with big titles. Don't be intimidated by a title.

Don't be intimidated by the expectations either. Companies expect the usual from the applicant: Bachelor's degree required, excellent organizational and communication skills, a polished professional image, prior sales and marketing background a plus, etc. These are common, superfluous expectations for simple jobs. Many administrative/clerical positions only require limited skills such as a command of the English language, typing, and the use of fax machines, telephones, computers and copiers that require no extensive education or intelligence.

Even children can learn how to use computers and smart phones. Our public education system should prepare every student for entry-level office jobs. Our high school graduates should be ready to enter the working world immediately and not be forced to hit the books for 4 more years to get a decent job. They should not be sentenced to a life sentence of poverty because they don't want to go to college.

We must remember that colleges are businesses. They make money from media networks and corporations with their athletic programs and rake in billions of our tax dollars from Congress. (earmarks) Even if you never attended college, you are paying for them. Many of them would be out of business if degrees were not required for so many jobs.

College dropouts, high school grads and high school dropouts can learn a job with training. The employer has little idea of the applicants abilities until he's actually on *the job*. Nevertheless, the degree demand for office/clerical and other so-called skilled positions continues. The real motive seems to be the denial of higher paying job opportunities to poorer Americans, those who can not afford "higher learning." Of course, if an applicant knows someone on "the inside" they can get the job with or without a degree. It's not what you know, but who you know.

In college, you'll read more books, hear more business terminology and theories, go on dates, join sororities and attend some binge drinking parties, but there is no substitute for experience and books do not teach it. A 22 year old fresh out of college with no work experience is not wise.

We must realize how simple and ordinary people are when placed in situations differing from their routines and chosen professions. For example, if you asked a woman with a law degree to perform jet engine repairs, her knowledge is incompatible with the task and the results would be unsatisfactory for the FAA and the passengers boarding in 30 minutes. If you asked a jet engine mechanic to represent you in court, you might be better off representing yourself. If you hired a computer science major for a construction job, the results could be disastrous. Carpenters, pipe fitters and electricians are skilled people. Working on a computer screen is one thing, working on a construction site under tight building codes is quite another. Now, take an office manager and place him on the front counter of a restaurant during a high volume lunch rush. He might be a savvy businessman when dealing with one or two clients in his comfortable chair or on speakerphone, but would he be able to deal with 100 hungry people in 60 minutes time with the same professional demeanor?

Just because you don't sit behind a desk does not mean you're unskilled. There are also many jobs that require stamina, toughness and yes, skill. Jobs like metal finishing, seafood processing, miners, personal trainers, concrete workers, pasta/bread makers, printing pressmen, movers, landscapers, etc. It's hard to imagine out of shape office workers lasting for long in jobs like these.

We all bring different skills, strengths and experiences into the economy. Am I saying that a cashier should make as much money as a doctor? No. But I don't want to see $10 an hour craftsmen and pilots (due to the pressures of the global economy) either. Our pyramid system must stop paying 6 or 7 figures to people who sit behind desks and peanuts to everyone else.

Employers will have to forgive those of us who were not born into a well to do family and were expected to be employed and our own man or woman by age 18, 19 or 20. And with wages the way they are, it's difficult for someone in their late teens/early twenties to work full-time, pay *their own bills* and go to college. Then of course, financing issues arise for young working class people because of little or no established credit and the wages of the entry-level job. Thus, the choice of which college to attend is limited. This is another ugly example of our repressive pyramid structure taking shape and segregating the children of the rich and the working classes. The rich girl graduates from a reputable university at age 22 or 23 and gets a cushy professional/management position, while the working class girl struggles with a juggling act of work and school. She attended a less expensive (less reputable) college or a community college and ultimately, she will report to the rich kid in the professional/management position.

People bring different skills to the workplace. There are individuals who have excellent mechanical skills, but mediocre people skills and vice versa. Both mechanical/technical and communication skills are vital to a business and the U.S. economy as a whole. But the pyramid only rewards a few with the handsome salaries (lawyers, politicians, athletes, principals, medicine, top management, accountants) and belittles others that also require a high(er) degree of skill and intelligence, but are viewed as "blue collar" or "not professional" such as mechanics, electricians, pilots, police officers, firefighters, teachers, welders, machinists and plumbers.

Supposedly, we are paid according to our skill level and how well we benefit or please society. We should know how a restaurant worker or late night convenience clerk can "please us" when our stomachs are growling or we're running out of gas in a remote area of our state. We should also know how well a firefighter or police officer can please us when our property is burning or stolen. Teachers can serve as *positive role models* for our children. We are certainly pleased to have electricity and plumbing in our homes and businesses. The vehicles we drive and the roads we travel on are built and maintained by skilled people. These individuals certainly please society.

The other excuse to keep wages low for so-called blue collar jobs is the skill level. (non-skilled, semi-skilled) However, many Americans lack the physical strength and endurance to perform them, so supply and demand applies. Imagine an old judge operating a jackhammer or a prissy secretary laying bricks. Putting in time and actually working are two different things. On a production line or construction site, *you work.*

You think fast and move fast or else! But people who sit behind desks for a living put in a lot of time. Some of it is easily spent attending to their own affairs like applying makeup, clipping/filing nails, sending emails to friends and lovers, chatting and gossiping, paying bills online, eating, drinking coffee, etc.

The working conditions are very different for professionals and blue collar workers as well. Sitting at a desk in an air conditioned/heated office provides a safe, comfy environment for executives.

Unfortunately, working conditions are often hazardous and uncomfortable for the blue collar workforce. We have human forklifts (people lifting and carrying tremendous weight) and human vacuum cleaners (people breathing harmful vapors and welding smoke) on the job is dusty and dangerous environments. The professionals and execs take their one hour meal breaks while workers have to wolf down their food and be back on the production line in 30 minutes. Workers should have 40-60 minutes for meal breaks and 20 minutes for rest periods. Maybe they can actually relax and chew their food with the extra time.

The changes I'm proposing, (fairer wages, cleaner work environments) are resisted fiercely by the professionals and the rich. Many blue-collar jobs are viewed as "non-core" or "non-value" positions that can be outsourced to temporary agencies or foreign hordes. Therefore, workers must revive union power. *Strong unions* and a pro-worker/family government (instead of a corporate controlled one) will restore a fair balance between business and labor, white collar and blue.

"Union" should not be a dirty word in America. Is there something wrong with a well paid workforce? The rich and their political/media allies have painted a distorted picture of unions as communist and under mafia tutelage. Union members have been branded as lazy hooligans. The unions never intended to overthrow the government and the capitalist system, they only fought for basic rights and capitalism with a human face. Thanks in large part to them, child labor was stopped and we receive paid vacations and time and a half for working over 40 hours a week. Without them, children would be working in coal mines and overtime pay would be abolished.

The rich have always feared the united strength

of workers and their tactics prove it. People have been beaten and murdered in this country for striking. The rich encourage the outsourcing of our jobs and lobby our government for more immigrants to provide plenty of scabs to breakup strikes. Illegal aliens are a sledgehammer in the hands of the rich to batter our unions and wages.

If you listen to pro-corporate fiction based on lowest common denominator logic, you'll hear about "$40 an hour union janitors" and hear that we actually haven't lost many manufacturing jobs. The only jobs sent overseas were "old skill" positions that our "advanced economy" no longer needs. (eight track tapes) But, I'm well aware of the date and time and the last time I looked, Americans still buy televisions, computers, automobiles, bicycles, beds, tables, clothing, sofas, dishes, lumber, plastics, steel, cement, boots, shoes and tires. These are in fact, high demand products and we need to start producing them in our own country. Wouldn't it be nice to have these jobs available when a recession hits and for people who need a second job? How about high school grads who need a job immediately to get their first apartment or students who want to gain *on the job experience?*

Unions need to continue the struggle for 21st century wages and stop donating to politicians who have not delivered on stopping anti-worker legislation. If you're taking the dues, earn them, and fight for the legal citizens who pay them. Unions are not a panacea, but a positive force for our working citizens, a shield against pro-corporate government and out of control globalization. Without unions, our middle class (what's left of it) will shrink and ultimately vanish. We'll be left with a ruling class, a tiny professional class and a peasant class.

Money

According to religious teachings, the rich are a scorned lot who can lose their fortunes overnight to theft, war, overindulgence or treachery. Divine punishment looms for them as they live their lives of lavish, pompous pleasure while the vast majority of their countrymen languish in poverty or mediocrity. So it is written, "The love of money is the root of all evil." Perhaps this is a partially true statement. Money is used for destructive purposes, from the bribery of politicians to contract murder. Money can tempt a man to commit a crime, tempt a lover to commit adultery, or tempt a nation to attack its neighbor. But ultimately, these decisions, these choices, lie with the responsible individual. You can *resist* these pressures for financial gain. You do not have to be enslaved or compromise your honor for it.

A similar scenario involves a firearm. A hitman has just raised a rifle and taken aim at his intended victim. A killing can take place, but he doesn't have to pull the trigger. If he does, he is a murderer and he will collect his payment, but if he lowers the weapon, he has triumphed over this urge for profit. Of course, we need money, we work for it and learn skills that enable us to earn more of it. We expect fair compensation for our labor, time, service or skill. Everything you own took someones labor, time, service or skill to create for you. Therefore, payment was necessary for every possession. That is why the root of all evil can actually be a lack of money, (poverty) particularly in a competitive and greedy society like the United States. How sweet can your life really be without a decent job? Your home, car, clothing and food all cost money.

It is said that "Money can't buy love." That is debatable too. How many women want to marry a poor man? How many seek a man who can't hold down a job and lives with his mother at age 30? Too many American women are materialistic to the core, conditioned by our consumer system and they don't want scrubs. But if Mr. Scrub suddenly won the state lottery or inherited a substantial sum of money, my how things would change!

Now, how many men want a gold digger who is spending his money faster than he can earn it because she has little or none of her own? You won't find many, unless he's filthy rich and two or three times her age. Old, wealthy men love young concubines to satisfy ego, status and the dream of being young again, even though the youth and vigor faded long ago. If his money was gone, she would be too. But he tries to convince himself that she loves him for his fatherly wit, maturity and distinguished good looks.

Money provides security. You can save your cash, draw interest and buy property. People are drawn to you when you have money and some of them will be flatterers, whores and parasites. But the vast majority do not have the distinction of being financially successful.

Less than 1 % of Americans are millionaires. The rest of us struggle day by day for survival and get frustrated and angry when hard work does little or nothing to improve our financial security. We work harder and longer, but our living standards do not improve. They worsen. Every day is a carbon copy of the last. Awaken, work, return home, sleep, awaken, go back to work. The dehumanizing daily grind goes on and on to the point where you are reduced to the level of a machine.

If the average American worker could see the future and see what's in store for him, he would be shocked and angry. If he could peer through the fog to the years ahead, he would still see himself chained to an enormous, rusted wheel. Hour after hour and day after day, he slowly moves this object, desperately scooping up the dollar bills and pocket change uncovered by its difficult movement. Decades pass and finally, he can move it no further. At last, he looks upward and raising his arms, he screams, "I can't go on! What do I have for my years of work? What belongs to me?" At that moment, a gigantic hand descends and lands on the ground next to him. It is the hand of our government and in its palm lies his reward for a lifetime of work and paying taxes. He gapes at the sight and falls to his knees. "No, it just can't be." he says with disgust.

Lying on the hand are the fruits of his labor: a sparsely furnished mobile home, a loaf of bread and a little social security check. The American Dream is now the American Nightmare. Wiping tears from his eyes, he asks, "Surely my children's future will be more promising, what will they reap for their work?" A new vision forms on the hand and the man's eyes widen with terror. Are you going to end up like him 20 or 30 years from now?

It is the plight of the American worker, who is overworked, overtaxed and underpaid by a cruel plutocracy deploying carrot and stick deceptions. The elite dangle the American Dream before our eyes and we race after the prize. But try as we may, it can not be attained. Our youth is spent, many of our best years are wasted chasing a fantasy. As we age, the pace slows and hope is lost. So we turn to television, alcohol and drugs to tune out the grim truth. Finally, old and broken, the pursuit ends. A decrepit retirement is in store now, far too brittle to challenge the establishment, we hope for its mercy and pray for our social security.

In the eyes of a greedy owner or CEO, his workforce is like a pack of dogs. Some are well fed, but most are thin and sickly. When the time comes to reward good behavior, the dogs will huddle around him and his big bag of snacks, anticipating a full stomach for a job well done. Unfortunately, only 2 or 3 of his favorites receive the best bites, while the rest of the pack receives only foul scraps and bones. Some of the dogs fight savagely among themselves even for the smallest of these prizes. Occasionally, the man will be angry with his dogs and some will have their food portions reduced, while others are banished to their doghouses for cold nights outside. When he loses his temper with them, he will replace them with more obedient pets. Of course, this is a cruel existence for the dogs, but they live in the man's home and are fed there. If they run away, they face the risk of being taken into a home that is crueler than the former. There is also the risk of not being taken into any home at all. These "strays" can be rounded up by animal control (the government) and detained. On the other hand, some strays find better homes. These owners apply primitive psychological reinforcements and punishments to teach the dogs "new tricks" (more productivity and obedience) instead of using a belt. This can also be an abusive environment, but the food is better here and there are more "bones" tossed their way.

Poverty is destructive, but excessive wealth can also be detrimental to human beings, to the point of megalomania. He no longer has any love for people or country, but only material possessions and power. He becomes mistrustful of family, friends, employees and business associates, believing they have no interest in his personality or companionship, but only in his financial power. The wealthy one, realizing this motive, will attempt to control the less fortunate person with his greater clout. Big money can certainly create a superiority complex that leads to isolation and arrogance because money is his only concern. More money is required for personal satisfaction, but *permanent satisfaction* and peace of mind are never realizied because more happiness constantly requires more money. When he has banked $500,000, it is not enough, now he wants $1,000,000, then $2,000,000, etc. This is simply greed.

While Mr. and Mrs. Rich show off expensive jewelry, fancy suits, new luxury cars and trips around the world, the average American worker can only muster a cheap wristwatch, faded jeans, a modest car still owned by the bank, and a "get away" to the nearest city park. The former lifestyle is the fantasy of easy living, wealth and power that we are constantly shown by the media. But the latter is the real America, the rat race of survival and getting ahead, but very few of us do.

The only way we will get ahead is with higher wages and tax cuts. Hitherto, many government tax schemes and corporate welfare have had a detrimental effect, because they have hidden and long term costs for the working classes.

It's the same old situation with the stock market, the global gambling casino of corporate empires. A few get filthy rich in it, but the working classes rarely benefit with their small 401k contributions and lack of Wall Street connections and are susceptible to the endless scandals (Bernard Madoff) orchestrated in the name of the free market. Then there are the wild claims about 401k performance. Just put aside 10% or so and you'll be a millionaire when you retire. Supposedly, this is where the economic "trickle down" theories take their course. But they don't. The big profits are hoarded by greedy bastards in overseas tax havens and bank accounts. The fat rats get fatter, but no one else benefits. The working classes have to settle for the usual, puny raises and daily bread. That's the real America, that's the real deal.

The Cold War and its Aftermath

The ideology of Karl Marx (1818-1883) and Friedrich Engels (1820-1895) mobilized the hopes of millions, from utopians to disgruntled factory workers. Marxism was a direct challenge to imperialism and worker exploitation, with the aim of freeing the masses from capitalism and class conflict. In Marx's image of the world, the wage earners (the proletariat) were the class of destiny. They would demand better wages and political power, which would lead to the removal of the privileged classes. (the bourgeoisie) New societies would rise within a community of socialist nations. At the socialist stage, a dictatorship of the proletariat would be necessary to control the means of production and prepare for the higher stage of communism. Once communism was achieved, the nation itself would be unnecessary and the world would be as one. Earth would not count on the blessings of a god for the "shining future" but rather, the blessings of science and technological progress.

Marx never lived to see his theories put to the test. Lenin, Trotsky, Stalin, Mao, Ho Chi Minh, Pol Pot, Kim Il-sung, Che Guevara and Castro have had their own modified interpretations of the ideology. Lenin's Soviet Union was the world's first socialist state. It was huge with abundant natural resources, but decimated by World War I. Lenin's "peace at any price" policy resulted in the 1917 treaty of Brest-Litovsk and humiliating defeat. Internal struggles between pro and anti-communist forces raged until 1922. Thus, the system was implemented in a wrecked and divided country and put at a huge disadvantage from the start.

Lenin's successor, Joseph Stalin, ruled the state with an iron fist. He was convinced that the USSR had to turn to industrialization and collectivization to make the nation strong and keep the capitalist powers from attacking again. Building more steel and war machines made it a leading industrial power and better prepared for war, but farming and consumer goods production suffered, causing starvation and misery among the people.

During the 1930s, Stalin unleashed the "Great Purge." Bureaucrats, intellectuals and military officers were executed or imprisoned on trumped up charges. Then his wrath was turned on anyone who was the slightest threat (real or imagined) to his Machiavellian rule. With the brutal massacre, exile and incarceration of millions, the country was terribly weakened again for the Nazi attack on June 22, 1941.

It is unlikely that any other nation could have endured the savage beating that the Soviet Union took from Hitler's armies during World War II. Millions were killed and injured, cities were demolished, industry and agriculture suffered catastrophic damage. But Hitler (like Napoleon) underestimated the toughness of his eastern enemy and the Soviets were victorious in the end, crushing German armies all the way back to Berlin. Its stubborn, valiant resistance earned it admiration and fear around the world. By 1950, it *seemed* stronger than it was prior to the war; Eastern Europe, including a large chunk of Germany itself was under Soviet influence.

It also possessed the atomic bomb. But the USSR was still bloodied and afraid of the American superpower. Relations quickly soured with the West and its resources were directed toward military buildups.

Under Khrushchev and Brezhnev, there were some successes. In 1957, the Soviets launched Sputnik 1, the first artificial satellite to orbit the earth. A greater accomplishment came four years later when the Soviets put the first man in space, Yuri Gagarin. In 1975, the Soviet Union boasted to the world that it had achieved nuclear parity with the United States. In the same year, the U.S. concluded its inglorious withdrawal from Vietnam, a defeat ensured in part by Soviet aid to communist Vietnamese forces and a defeat that marks what many believe is the origin of American decline. The Soviet Union looked like a success on the international stage, but this confidence led to a disastrous war in 1979 with the invasion of Afghanistan.

Even before the invasion, Soviet resources were already stretched to the breaking point. Its economy was inefficient and suffered from incompetent central planning. The country could produce thousands of tanks and missiles and construct enormous concrete apartment blocks, but finding comfortable clothing and fresh vegetables in the stores was a daily challenge. Soviet propaganda and "socialist realism" portraying smiling, well fed workers in a socialist heaven denied reality and dissent was growing.

As the leader of the communist world, it was obliged to finance "liberation movements" around the globe. It had to match the military challenge of NATO and keep order among its many nationalities and in its eastern European satellites. Moscow also cast a suspicious eye on its lengthy border with China; guarding it and protecting Mongolia from possible Chinese aggression caused another massive drain on manpower and resources. In 1981, the Solidarity movement threatened Soviet interests in Poland. When Brezhnev died in 1982, the USSR was an overextended, armed camp.

The next Soviet leader, Yuri Andropov, attempted some reforms to reduce corruption and improve efficiency. When Andropov died in 1984, Konstantin Chernenko succeeded him. Under Chernenko, the Soviet Union boycotted the 1984 Summer Olympics in Los Angeles, an apparent payback for the U.S. boycott of the 1980 Summer Olympics in Moscow. After 13 months in office, Chernenko died in 1985. At last, Mikhail Gorbachev came to power and with his policies of glasnost and perestroika, the fear of the Soviet people inherited from Stalin's time diminished along with the outside NATO threat. When it became clear that there was really no *threat* from the West and there would be no crackdown from Moscow for disobedience, the USSR and the Warsaw Pact quickly fell apart.

So was the Soviet Union really a threat to America? Looking back on the Cold War, it is clear that it was a legitimate threat to America's security and leading position in the 1950s and 1960s. The threat became all too real in October of 1962, when a Soviet missile buildup in Cuba was revealed. For over a week, the world stood on the brink of a nuclear war as the superpowers hammered out a compromise to end the crisis. Finally, Kennedy announced to a nervous American public that the Soviet missile bases were being dismantled.

In the 1970s, the Soviet economy was rotting from corruption and inefficiency, but kept alive by oil profits. By 1980, the Soviet threat was over, its invasion of Afghanistan the last heave, but right-wing rhetoric in America continued the hype.

The exaggerated Soviet threat and fear mongering was quite simply, a con job orchestrated by the U.S. government and corporate interests to "justify" enormous military budgets. The media and Hollywood got in on the act, releasing movies like "War Games", "The Day After" and "Red Dawn" as if a Soviet nuclear attack or invasion was imminent. Reagan's 1983 "evil empire" speech was another dose of exaggeration for the public, as if the USSR was stronger than ever. This was simply not the case. But many Americans believed it and this fear contributed to Reagan's re-election in 1984 and ensured "4 more years" of bloated military budgets to "catch up" with the "evil empire."

Conservatives argue that Reagan's defense spending broke the Soviets. They overlook Pope John Paul II's support of the Solidarity movement, the 1986 Chernobyl disaster, Mikhail Gorbachev's reforms, declining oil revenues, nationalist movements within the USSR and overextension.

As the 21st century progresses, Marxist governments continue to disappear or adhere to the ideology only in name. China, Cuba, Vietnam, North Korea and Laos remain as socialist states with authoritarian or totalitarian styles of government, antagonistic attitudes toward the United States and the usual propaganda glorifying its leaders. But with the demise of the Soviet Union, even these holdouts have faced facts and they are controlled by thugs who have too much to lose by admitting that the system doesn't work. They blame the United States or their own people instead of the system.

The social and economic theories of Marx have failed. It is a utopian idea that contributed to the deaths of millions. Those who make the claim that authentic Marxism was never attempted, must understand that it wouldn't have mattered even if it was. Creating a society of robots is not the answer. There is some consolation for Marxist theory. Adam Smith's obsolete raw capitalism is not the answer either. His economic theories have caused slavery, plutocracy, poverty and fraud. The 21st century has proven them both wrong.

In America, there are still some small, financially strapped groups like the Freedom Socialist Party and the Communist Party of the United States of America. Some radical minorities and left-wing Democrats still embrace Marxist principles. Consequently, many of its American adherents are feminists and homosexuals, who have hijacked the ideology as their own, reducing its appeal to a wider audience.

After the dissolution of the Soviet Union and

the Warsaw Pact, America stood tall on the international stage as the one and only superpower. With this "new world order" came a change in American foreign policy; more attention was shifted from Europe to Asia.

Diplomacy with China has been a challenge as the PRC strives for more influence in Asia and around the world. America's policy toward China is schizophrenic. We grant China most favored nation trading status and at the same time, ridicule Beijing's human rights record and rising military spending. America has defended Taiwan's autonomy, yet China claims that the island is a renegade province that should be under its administration. The 2001 Hainan Island incident and 2009 South China Sea incident increased tensions between the Pacific giants.

China and the United States can not bully one another, so the "partnership" is strictly business and one of convenience as each side exploits trade agreements. China needs jobs for its masses and export markets. The U.S. wants cheap products for its consumers and China provides them (of suspect quality) to the delight of our corporations, that use Chinese soil as foreign districts of operations. American workers are not competing with Chinese companies, they're competing with Chinese workers on corporate America's pay-roll. The corporations themselves are the "competition" and China is used to apply pressure on Americans to work for less. Our corporations are strengthening a rival that could eat us alive in the near future. This is a senseless policy that has weakened our industrial base and shoved millions into unemployment lines at home. But CEOs only care about profits, even if they endanger our leading position by helping Beijing.

Our government could restrain these outsourcing traitors by limiting commerce with the PRC, but instead, it has done what their corporate sponsors demand, by removing trade barriers, giving tax breaks to offshore and allowing "free trade" with the authoritarian state. Beijing and Washington use each other for economic reasons, but their political differences can cause friction at any moment.

The Korean peninsula remains a trouble spot for U.S. diplomacy. North Korea and its "million man army" has resisted the tide of change that swept over the Soviet Union, eastern Europe and to a lesser extent, China. Stalinist discipline remains in place and hostility towards America,

Japan and its southern neighbor continues. Approximately 28,000 U.S. troops remain in South Korea to deter the communist North from an invasion attempt. North Korea's broken promises to halt its nuclear weapons program have been a source of frustration and fear in the region. In 1993, it became the first nation to withdraw from the Nuclear Nonproliferation Treaty, an international pact designed to stop the spread of nuclear weapons. Pyongyang suspended the withdrawal, but in 2002, the North admitted to a secret nuclear weapons program. In 2003, North Korea withdrew indefinitely from the Nonproliferation Treaty. Six nation talks involving China, Russia, Japan, North Korea, South Korea and the United States have failed to resolve the crisis.

North Korea's 2006 and 2009 nuclear tests proved that the regime can not be trusted and raised questions about who is really in charge of the country. Its blackmailing of the world continues.

America doesn't want another Korean War, so the region requires complicated and cautious diplomacy. If more harsh sanctions are applied, the North might lash out with an underfunded, aging military still capable of wreaking havoc and death on the peninsula. If the U.S. does nothing, then the North may build more nuclear weapons, longer range missiles to deliver them, and export nuclear materials. It's a trap and the North knows it. America is hoping that the country will crumble internally and sweep the tyrannous regime from power. Its primitive economy is dependent on foreign aid and many North Koreans are supposedly starving. So Washington will fan any flames of discontent within the country and lean on its economy, but gently, and only with help from regional players like China, Japan and Russia. It seems like a cowardly policy, but a reckless course could lead to disaster and more U.S. commitments. Without its military, North Korea would have no significance on the world stage. Its prospects for survival are slim.

Japan is an economic superpower, but remains under treaty restrictions from her World War II defeat. Consequently, Japan can not build a mighty military machine, even though she is quite capable of doing so. This restriction on military spending actually contributed to the success of its economy. While the United States was squandering billion on wars and military buildups during the Cold War, Japan rapidly developed a powerful economy. The "imitators" became the imitated as Japanese companies gained market share and an international reputation for high quality products. During the 1980s, American companies seemed to forget the basics of quality and customer service, compromising both for flashy marketing gimmicks and excessive management salaries. The American worker and unions served as scapegoats for failed corporate strategies, a blame game that returned in 2009 with the bankruptcy of General Motors. Despite U.S. criticism of Japan's restrictive import policies (protectionism) and a rare U.S. tariff on Japanese products, the immense trade between the two nations continues, swelling the profits of Japanese corporations and increasing American trade deficits.

If Japan was allowed to develop its armed forces, it could rival American and Chinese influence in the region. In the coming decades, Japan may shake off its American protectorate status and pursue a course more befitting of a world power. In the face of threats from North Korea and the growing power of China, it may have no choice.

Vietnam is another country that America has been paying special attention to. In 1994, the U.S ended a 19 year trade embargo on the country.

The U.S. extended full diplomatic recognition in 1995. These actions caused resentment at home among some Vietnam veterans and conservatives. But its 85 million inhabitants make a potentially lucrative market and work site for American jobs, so corporations are scrambling to reap the profits. Sure enough, the U.S. and Vietnam signed a comprehensive trade deal in 2000. Improved relations between the former enemies could serve as a counterweight to Chinese ambitions in the future.

Corporate Clones

Regardless of your financial status, you must face life everyday. Whether you're rich, upper middle class, middle class, wage earner or poor, people form strong and immediate opinions of an individual based on appearance and material possessions. Even though a book should not be judged by its cover, people are.

How do you feel when you commute in a worn out car and move through intersections among shiny new ones driven by sophisticated looking people? How would you feel if you entered a restaurant in jeans and a T-shirt, while the rest of the patrons are dressed well enough to attend an opera, wearing business suits, tuxedos and gowns? What you may sense is a feeling of inadequacy or inferiority, while a sense of superiority is felt by the woman in the sedan and the man in the tuxedo as they glance at your car and clothes. No words are exchanged, no physical attack, but psychologically, your face is slapped by these snobs.

Your co-workers are well aware of your position in the business and the measure of respect you receive from them is influenced by it. If you're a temp or other low wage associate, you mingle with the other temps and low wage associates because you share a lower social class. Even entire cities are financially segregated. The rich live in their gated communities and high rises, the professionals live in their comfortable houses with mountain and waterfront views, the middle and wage earners live in crowded suburban neighborhoods and apartment buildings, and the poor live in trailer parks, housing projects, or on the street.

When you shop for food or clothing, do you go to finer department stores or less reputable ones? Do you shop at second-hand stores? Either way, you can be judged by others as you select merchandise and load your shopping cart. People notice what kinds of clothing and jewelry you wear. You can't escape these perceptions in a materialistic society. It is the great evil of American materialism, judging a human being by his possessions and not by his virtues. These primitive attitudes diminish the unity and decency of our country.

Immorality is a bastard son of materialism. Husbands and wives will dump their partners for a wealthier lover so fast the victim's head will spin. For example, if you're involved in an "open marriage" arrangement and your wife's boss makes a lot more money than you, the result is predictable. In this society, you can rarely trust your spouse or partner if you're struggling financially, because you are in danger of sinking to a lower social class. Of course, this behavior is shameful and wrong, but greed and immorality are intertwined. To keep up with the "Joneses" and "move up", marriages (and children) have suffered. Do you believe that your husband or wife would reject a date with his/her CEO or a celebrity for the sake of your commitment?

If he/she is a decent person, they would indeed, but with this impossible financial system, precious few would allow an opportunity for a promotion/increased social status to pass them by, regardless of their affection for you.

It is unfortunate that *anyone* gains fame,

fortune and promotions for risque and downright sleazy behavior. Instead of being rewarded for intelligence, talent and merit, glory is heaped on the scum of our society. The fascination with pop culture icons and the idle rich is transforming our young people into corporate clones. The message is: be sexy and go after the money. We expect the judgment of 8-18 year olds to withstand the corporate marketing and peer pressures of society. We must not forget that impressionable youth and young adults can be led astray and corrupted by negative role models and fads that are *corporate props*. Corporations are only concerned with sales, not the well being of our young people, who are the future of our country. If the young are ruined, America is ruined.

This system manipulates and poisons the struggling majority, distracting us with television, materialism and sex. The rich and their corporate marketers establish behavior standards and we are expected to follow. Through their control of the media, they show us "what's in" regarding music and fashion. We're always shown skinny, smiling people with perfect teeth using their products. You're not with it or a loser if you don't behave like their actor or don't buy their product.

They establish what the ideal American man and woman should be. These perverted pressures are exerted on us everyday. This herd mentality brings enormous wealth to corporations and sleazy celebrities and creates rebellious youth, promiscuity and dysfunctional families among the masses.

Destructive and promiscuous behaviors are notoriously celebrated by the media. "Who is that pop star sleeping with this week?" "That actor got arrested again!"

"Those women kissed each other!", and so on. Immediately after the media buzz surrounding the incident, the celebrity announces the release of a new album or book. The method: create controversy and cash in on it.

American promiscuity is impossible to precisely calculate, but bluntly obvious in the country. Flirtatious advances, (whether married or not) provocative clothing worn in public, multiple partners and prostitution are lifestyle traits embraced by millions in one form or another. The media presents it all as insignificant behavior, (everyone does it) as if we're a bunch of subhumans with no self-control or decency.

To a materialistic, immoral woman, a marriage even with children involved, has little significance. There is little or no effort on her part to repair a troubled marriage, to rekindle romantic passions or improve communication. Little or no effort to do her best each day for her children, as *all parents* must do without exception. Instead, she views the husband as a "paycheck dad", a sucker to pay her bills and provide the illusion of a normal family. "Sexual freedom" is executed to the fullest behind the husband's back to satisfy grotesque fantasies encouraged by feminist/fashion magazines by sleeping with other women, scoring "points" at work by sleeping around with the "higher ups" and engaging in interracial flings to confirm sexual myths.

It is cherished by high maintenance women (and hookers) above all other things, the almighty dollar. Even the ugliest, old man can have a young, beautiful woman ... if he's rich ... In her quest for the "best man", (stressed by mothers to their daughters at the tenderest age) she is on alert for the successful looking man to latch on to. What kind of shoes does he wear? What kind of car does he drive? What kind of job does he have? Does he have a college degree?

For this materialistic one, a poor man is not in the plan. As a gold digger, she'll waste little time showing interest in a man with money. From the first date, she will swiftly calculate what this sucker is really worth, from the dinner and tip, to the cologne he's wearing and the side of town he lives in. It's a shrewd assessment of her next meal ticket. You can almost see the dollar signs in her eyes.

If he measures up to her financial standards, she'll give him her number and hint about a more serious encounter on the next date. Of course, this means a chance of "getting in her pants" so the man is almost certain to follow up. On the other hand, if his lifestyle does not measure up, he will be swiftly dismissed. This is done in a variety of ways. She may simply refuse to be seated at a restaurant that does not satisfy her taste or refuse to get in his vehicle if it is not a luxury sedan or sports car. She might let the date conclude, but reject any offers for another; "I'm too busy." "I found someone else." "Let me think about it." typical responses that mean she's not interested in going on with the relationship.

Another odd phenomenon is the demasculinization of men. This "trend" encourages men to be softer and in touch with their feelings and so-called "feminine side." Thus, we have limp-wristed men cleaning house and watering flowers on television, while the feminist superwoman brings home the bacon and wears the pants in the family. It seems like left-wingers and their media allies are at war with the nuclear family and the alpha male. Strong men scare the feminists and gays in Hollywood, the thought of a John Wayne society is apparently threatening. So instead, we have men acting like girls on television. They're indecisive and nonathletic. The "modern man" portrayed by the media is not a man at all, only a spineless geek.

The media's fascination with tomboy feminism is obvious in the country, contributing to resistance against the traditional, nurturing role of women. The mother/housewife role is rejected and belittled. Stay at home moms are branded as losers.

In the workplace, demands by feminists for promotions is never ending and if they are *genuinely deserved,* more power to them. But it doesn't end there. There are demands for *women only businesses* and more women in leading managerial roles, solely because of their gender, not because of *ability,* which is outright sexual discrimination. Since women only earn 75-85 cents for every dollar that a man makes, (calculations differ substantially by source) the call to level the field and dispose of the dreaded "glass ceiling" goes on. They conveniently forget that both genders are exploited by this nepotistic system. Radical N.O.W. feminists have divided American workers. The struggle for fair wages and bright futures is not a woman only issue. It concerns *all Americans* who are not achieving well deserved success.

Today, women play an equal (or dominant) role in many professions: the media, teaching, administration, banking, sales, health care, customer service, etc. Government and union jobs are well represented by women. Even traditionally male dominated positions like construction trades, law enforcement, truck drivers and engineering are being filled by women. The armed forces are open to female participation. They even have their own professional sporting leagues to cheer for. The gender gap has been blown out of proportion by man hating activists.

Men and women are different and have contributed to history differently.

Despite PC/feminist attempts to rewrite history, (herstory) the past can not be changed.

Instead of planning for the honorable role of motherhood, feminists want to prove how "powerful" they are.

Supposedly, the mother/housewife role will reduce the woman to a weaker status. In the feminist/media view, the ideal American "womyn" is childless, androgynous and single. If she wants a male mate, she can proceed, but he must understand that "she's in charge" and the wimpier he is, the better. Men are seen as pigs or wimps, so wimps are preferred.

To be feminine is "passe" now, a throwback to a time when fertility rates were high and the man was the breadwinner. In the eyes of the law, we are equal, but in the eyes of nature, we are opposite sexes. But to feel "equal" to men, there is the perverted desire to act like men. Great damage has been done to the nation's children as a result and we should be fully aware of the atrocities committed by mothers on their own children, which include beatings, neglect and murder. They regret having children at all, wishing they never had them. They'd rather be one of the "strong and independent" feminist fanatics they idolize.

The peculiarities of left-wing thought have produced an inconsistent social ideology that is hazardous to a decent society. The Left pleads for mercy and rehabilitation for criminals, instead of justice for victims. They pity child molesters, cop killers, death row inmates and laboratory animals, but have no concern for unborn children. The Left tolerates all religions, even radical Islam and wacky cults, but not Christianity. Liberals revere the Constitution, but strongly support the "right" to burn the American flag. According to liberals, minorities are never racist, only white people are. Their struggle for equality has rarely included white males or Asian-Americans.

Their assault on the American nuclear family is despicable. Feminism is the primary weapon against families. It is promoted to spread rebellion against the woman's traditional roles of wife and mother. Among its most radical adherents, you will discover claims that *any* sexual intercourse is rape and a man who stares at a woman has committed a "mini rape." If men and women do not procreate, our population will age, decline and die out. Nevertheless, many feminists wish to be childless and they aggressively promote the single, childless lifestyle in our country as an ideal for the "modern woman." The alternative of artificial insemination is also promoted, so the feminist can raise a child without the unwanted influence of a father. Children suffer without a father figure, a nanny or girlfriend is a poor substitute.

These "wimmin" will flaunt their figures in public, yet they are quick to file sexual harassment charges. They want their own institutions and empowerment programs, yet they demand the right to enter all male institutions for the sake of "equality." Their lifestyle must be automatically accepted and not ridiculed in the workplace. If she's "offended" by something you say, this can cost you your job and cost the business a large sum of money from a "discrimination lawsuit." The melancholy, shoulder chipped attitude is unattractive. The hyper insecurity and nagging is a turnoff. No wonder American men go shopping for partners in the Philippines, Eastern Europe and Latin America. They find women who aren't all about themselves and even know how to cook.

The televised trash of Jerry Springer, Ricki Lake and others magnified the country's immoralities and justified them with roars of applause from an ultra-liberal studio audience. Sleazy programs like these cash in on America's illnesses by promoting feminism, homosexuality and incest. Traditional decency is always questioned, which creates a tolerance, then acceptance of anti-family and misfit lifestyles, very effective propaganda to influence the minds of our young people.

Left-wingers have vigorously defended abortion on demand rights as well, sending the wrong messages to impressionable girls with "it's my body" and "it's my choice" slogans. They even demonize the unborn, utilizing quack science claiming that a fetus or partially developed infant is "not a human being." The Left is guilty of encouraging girls to dispose of newborns if abortion is forbidden by the parents or unavailable, and defending girls who have murdered or abandoned their babies.

Throwing babies in garbage cans or rivers is somehow excusable to them.

Parents should certainly have a say in whether their juvenile daughter has an abortion or not. The biological father should also be heard. But the Left has no regard for parent or fathers rights and no regard for the life evolving inside of women.

Right-wingers have taken an extreme stance on this issue as well. Their basic argument is that the unborn must be protected because abortion is murder and a sin. Some hardcore conservatives have taken it upon themselves to enforce "God's will" by attempting to prevent abortions from being performed. In their eyes, it is justifiable to bomb clinics and murder abortion doctors. Both sides represent views that are far too extreme for most Americans to sympathize with. Where is the moderate path?

The debate on this hot button issue goes on. Should the procedure be permitted unconditionally, banned completely or allowed under special circumstances? Should it be allowed as a last resort? What do we expect a woman to do if she is raped? After the rapist is released from prison, should he be granted custody/visitation rights and allowed to return to the scene of the crime to pickup his son or daughter? Who would have the unenviable task of telling the kid how he/she came into this world and how would the child react? Or would the parents have to live a lie, always wondering if the other parent and family members have kept their silence?

If abortion is banned, people will have it done in other countries and more newborns will be placed under the care of the State, where they may or may not be adopted. We will find more newborns on the front steps of churches and in garbage cans. Abortion is a controversial, divisive issue and often abused, but it must be an option in cases of rape and incest and when complications during pregnancy threaten the life of the mother. It should also be an option when severe deformities are discovered and it becomes obvious that the child would be unable to function mentally and/or physically. These conditions represent a moderate approach to abortion.

Donkeys and Elephants

Whether you're interested in politics or not, the two major parties, the Democrats and Republicans, dominate the process from the highest office in the land to the local bureaucratic positions. With few exceptions, America's course is directed by the donkeys and elephants. There are a few independents, Tea Partyers, (repackaged Republicans) socialists and reformers, but none pose a serious challenge to the dual party control of the system. With so much agitation for "change" in the country, it is surprising that smaller parties have not grown and seated more members in congress or groomed legitimate contenders for the presidency. After all, the system is supposed to be by the people and for the people.

But power is monopolized by these behemoths so thoroughly that one or both can crush any serious challenge by a new party to alter the balance of power in Washington or its 50 state capitals. To attempt this would be like starting a new merchandising company and going head to head with Wal-Mart and Target. The companies with the far greater resources will win and unfortunately, the business of politics is no different in this era of bought elections. We have to understand that *real* socio-economic change will never occur while Democrats and Republicans hold complete power. Both use every gimmick to convince you that they're on your side and they're the party of change. But it's all a sham and 2 years after you voted them in, the system is exactly the same as it was on election day.

The GOP (Guarding Old Privileges) and their Tea Party allies generally believe that the free market and entrepreneurial capitalism will ensure prosperity. Their conservative philosophy stresses self-reliance as opposed to reliance on the government, because each and every one of us should be able to develop our God given abilities to the fullest without government interference. Sounds great doesn't it? But this is the same party that resists any attempt to raise the minimum wage with hollow claims that increasing it "kills jobs" (as if offshoring doesn't) It has attacked unions, siding with business interests. The GOP uses "big government" as an excuse to attack desperately needed "interference" programs like social security, welfare and medicare. The cuts in these programs are diverted to fund *corporate welfare* and enormous tax breaks for the wealthiest Americans. The Republicans frown on modernizing our lackluster health care system, branding these efforts as "socialism", "Hillarycare", or "Obamacare." In their perfect world, everyone owns a business, weakly regulated (or unregulated) by a corporate government. They seem to believe that if you don't own a business, you're a second class citizen or a loser in this boundless land of opportunity. People who don't make "six figures" should be very cautious about voting for the Republicans.

Christians should also be cautious about voting for them. For decades, the GOP has claimed the moral high ground, but free market greed and Christian teachings really have nothing in common. There are winks and nods to the Christian Right, but very little *action*. The Republicans have simply not delivered on issues like school prayer, abortion, traditional marriage, border security and the death penalty. Either nothing has changed or they are losing ground on every one of them.

The philosophy of the Democrats can be as destructive as the GOP's, but with a twist. They have a slightly better track record of protecting the workforce by defending unions, protecting social programs and fighting for minimum wage increases. But they go too far, requiring hefty tax increases to finance foreign aid handouts and bureaucracy. They generally believe that the government must *provide* equality and financial freedom. Unfortunately, reverse discrimination has evolved from this mentality. The government is expected to compensate for the crimes of the rich and people who are no longer with us. The tax and spend party is notorious for weak foreign policy and *excessive* defense cuts. They are also responsible for irresponsible immigration policies. Counting future votes, they want to open the floodgates of our country to just about anyone, from just about anywhere who wants a bite of our American pie. Democratic handouts are waiting to assist the legal and illegal aliens with housing, medical care, a college education and loans. Just like that, the immigrant can have a convenience store and a college degree. As the vanguards of extreme liberalism, the Democrats can not be

trusted any more than their Republican counterparts. Both have bizarre agendas.

In economic matters, the country has taken
a corporate right turn and in social matters, an
"anything goes" left turn. It is the worst of both
worlds. The country is stuck in a fiscally conservative, socially liberal course.

A congressional candidate can talk about
change, he/she can promise you better jobs and
schools, but the results are always the same. The
more things "change" the more they stay the
same. The rich stay rich (and get richer) and the
poor stay poor. The workers fight for survival or
join the ranks of the poor, dependant and incar-
cerated. Crime and drug problems continue and
public schools remain underfunded. The neighborhoods you avoid at night (or anytime) remain
avoided. Even if your city received some funds to
build a new park in that "bad area" with a jogging
path and swings for kids to play on, no one takes
their children in there or goes for a run without
a companion or weapon. It's one thing to build
and quite another to maintain what is built, to
preserve our public properties. When the maintenance funds are cut by the next mayor, the place
deteriorates and turns into a hangout littered with

beer bottles and graffiti. The area around the park is exactly the same, with the same gloomy, run-down apartments and battered houses. The same low paying or non-existent jobs trap the frustrated inhabitants and the same people just reclaim what's on their turf.

At work, you've seen some modest raises over the years, but only because of your own actions. You put in the overtime and do your job well. The people you vote for don't give you a raise, that's between you and the people who run the company. So you keep working hard and keep taking what they're giving. But every time your earnings grow, the rent, taxes and credit card interest rates seem to follow suit. You're still not living in that comfortable house or condo you were confident of having 3 or 4 years ago and you're still driving that same old car you vowed to replace with a newer one.

You still come home to the same old furnishings and rest on a bed made in the 1990s with stains on one side of the mattress, covered by a sheet and long since deodorized, but still there nonetheless. You still haven't taken that vacation you wanted to take 2 years ago either. America awaits you, but lack of money and time restricts you. The years keep rolling by, but it's just not getting done.

Your wardrobe is a bit larger, you have more shirts, jeans and socks. But many of your clothes are for work and since they're your best, you end up wearing these at home and on weekends away from your job. Sometimes, you save enough cash (instead of using a credit card) to buy new threads and hurry home with the shopping bags. The stuff looks good on you and they are proudly added to the chest of drawers and closet. But a few months later, most of the goods have been discarded or are seldom worn and moved to the end of the closet rack or placed in the bottom drawer of your chest. One of the shirts faded after a few washings and now it's only good as a "shop rag" or housecleaning shirt. Another shirt shrunk and it's uncomfortable. One pair of pants makes your butt look too big and another developed a hole the size of a dime on the crotch after a few washings and games of bowling. The quality just isn't there because of the export of our jobs, the clothes are made in foreign sweatshops.

Then you wonder why you bought some of this stuff to begin with. This product was supposed to make you look thinner and that product was supposed to make you more popular. You fell for another corny, corporate fad telling you how to dress and groom yourself. Soon after you buy the stuff, you are told that those products "are out" and now you must buy the new styles. The money is rarely there to keep up with these fads or to buy the *quality clothes* that *you really want* and nothing has really changed.

Despite the dual party fiscally conservative and socially liberal stagnation that prevents significant change in the country, there are few restraints on federal enforcement of law and order and how it responds to internal and external challenges. The abuses of government power are not limited to Kent State, Waco, Ruby Ridge and lies about Iraq's weapons of mass destruction. These are blundering, obvious examples, but there are others not widely acknowledged. The Right and the Left are guilty of implementing destructive economic and social agendas. This begins in the classrooms to shape the minds of our children. They are taught that America's economy is the best and there is opportunity and justice for all. They are taught a manipulated, politically correct history at an age when adult "wisdom" is absorbed and believed to be the absolute truth. Instead of demonizing Christopher Columbus and blaming all human atrocities on Western Europe, let us not erase from history the brutal conquests of the Mongols, the Ottoman invasion of Europe, Japan's World War II atrocities, Pol Pot's genocide, ethnic slaughter in Rwanda, Burundi and Indonesia and the thug regime of Idi Amin just to name a few. Intellectual honesty has been replaced with enormous oversimplifications and the PC demand, question it and you're denounced as a racist or xenophobe.

When the public education is complete (or not) and these young people enter the working world, most find low paying jobs and the struggle is on to be self-sufficient. They are reminded by politicians and the corporate media that this economic system is superior and there is *always* opportunity. So, the people blame themselves instead of economic and political forces beyond their control. Their poverty must be their own fault. After all, according to statistics and corporations, we are living in a land of milk and honey.

The high school grads and dropouts wonder if they should have gone to college and the people with two year degrees wonder if they should have taken out another big loan for a four year degree.

Those with bachelor's degrees wonder if a master's or PhD will improve their chances, even if this means educating themselves beyond their intelligence and financial means. They may blame their own parents for their humble status. They may blame it on their drinking or children, but rarely is the system blamed.

To remind the struggling vast majority of *their* failures, they are shown the fabulous, fairy-tale wealth of the tiny American elite on television and in movie theaters. Their noses are rubbed in *their* failures when they compare their own neighborhoods to the gated communities and mansions and their meager possessions to those of "successful" Americans. Compare and lash yourself. A class complex sets in and they generally associate only with people of their own social status. Frustration sets in when modest financial ambitions (a raise or promotion) are stonewalled. Depression arrives with alcohol/drug abuse and suicide. (to tune out reality) They keep blaming themselves and depression turns to outrage when they notice people from other countries enjoying taxpayer financed success in America. The people who should have the best opportunities are passed up by invaders.

But the government and the elite are well fed and they like the way things are in the country. They need a submissive herd and grateful immigrants to accept their system. (socialism for the rich and raw capitalism for the rest) They don't want to see an attempt by the American people to change their established order. They will do just about anything to keep their powers and privileges, including the deception of the people they're supposed to serve. Surely, many people realize that the country is not as prosperous as the government statistics say. According to the stats, very few of us are struggling and underemployed, economic problems exist in a few, small areas, but everyone else is prospering. Of course, it's all a pack of lies, but the system is *never* at fault, it's *always your fault.*

When a brave few demand real change or expose government abuse, the politicians turn to the media and label the reformers as "racists." When people challenge the corporate/right-wing dominance of our economy, they're labeled as "nativists", "anarchists", "socialists" or "communists." When people criticize the left-wing demolition of American culture, they're labeled as "rabble-rousers", "homophobes" or "xenophobes." We the people have the absolute right to question government performance, but that right is being forgotten and neglected, the government is questioning our right to question it, as if they always know what's best for us. To prevent any changes to the socially liberal, fiscally conservative status quo, the millions who suffer under it must be kept quiet and divided.

Unless you're a millionaire or billionaire, the American economy is a wreck and a bad joke. It is an economy inflated with Wall Street magic tricks, speculation and lies. Americans dread retirement, wondering if social security will be there. No one can save anything because wages are flat and trade and consumer debt is out of control. But our government announces dubious statistics to conceal or downplay economic reality. Enron did the same thing on their tax forms and balance sheets, their "official figures" were rubbish. But our politicians who live in a dream world reinforced with sham statistics are obsessed with showing the world its ideal society, claiming it is a model for all nations with its rampant crime, material gratification and moral decline. Exporting foul rap music and fast food is somehow proof of our cultural superiority.

Via satellite and DVD, Hollywood is shown on the television sets of people around the world. And what do they see? The same things Americans are shown; the family, religion and self-discipline are not important. They are shown the usual mansions, sports cars, sex, millionaire athletes, feminism and violence. The U.S. can interfere in the internal affairs of other countries without firing a shot by stirring up discontent in their citizens, particularly the young and rebellious.

For example, an Iraqi or Saudi woman watches the way American women behave (on television) and the way they dress in public. She will see an exaggerated success and impertinence. Now, she may question her own reliance on her husband and even question her home dress code which often requires a head covering and loose garments. Naturally, the American behavior on television is contrary to traditional, Islamic standards and problems arise, contributing to hatred of the United States and its decadent, intrusive culture. In the Islamic world, it is widely believed that our government and Hollywood are controlled by Jews. This explosive mixture of corporate morals (money is God and anything goes) combined with local customs is the root of Islamic extremism.

In China, a teenager sees an American businessman on the screen with his beachfront condo, fancy car and executive job.

It all seems so easy there! When the show is over, he will look at his own possessions, a bicycle and a one room shack with no running water and ask himself, "Why can't I live like American?" He is a prime candidate to do one of two things. 1. Push for change in the Chinese system or 2. Immigrate to the United States. (legally or illegally)

At first, this may appear to be a useful tool to destabilize the internal order in countries that our government wants to change, to steer them in a more capitalist and democratic direction. America absorbs into its own population, people from all continents who want the lifestyle they see on television. The problem is, it's all a bunch of lies. What they're seeing are actors and stage props. They never see people at work, sitting in traffic, paying bills and struggling to survive. Instead, they see a lifestyle that 1% of Americans actually have. Another problem with this interference is this: do we really have any business challenging the morals and traditions of independent countries with Jerry Springer values?

Is this part of an American scheme to dominate the world? Or is it target marketing by corporations that want to dump more of their products on the developing world? The corporations would love to make all Arabs, Africans and Chinese dress, eat and think like Americans. Like buzzards circling over carcasses, the multi-nationals want to get their claws into these markets and couldn't care less about their customs or morals. They only care about the host's natural resources, cheap labor and sales to its inhabitants.

World unity may be an impossible task, beyond the capacity of any nation or for that matter, the United Nations, but corporations want it all. They all want to go global because they see dollar signs in every country. *Their greed has no boundaries.* Human beings share the same globe, but we *do not* have identical interests. Marx never understood this and neither does our government. Based on crude, lowest common denominator logic, we're all simply humans or tailless apes, when in fact, we are many diverse groups with different religions, governments, histories, languages, customs and morals. We must acknowledge and respect them or nationalism will crush those who choose to play the role of God.

Corporate economics and San Francisco values have transformed America into a society of extremes. Do we really want our country dominated by new age hippies and CEOs? The Left's anti-Christian, pro-illegal alien, pro-feminist and soft on crime philosophy is poison for our social values. The Right's anti-union, pro-corporate and plunder the environment philosophy is poison for our standard of living.

Sometimes, the Left and Right form a partnership for their mutual benefit, an unholy alliance. The immigration issue provides evidence of this collaboration. The Left sees future votes when aliens pour into the country (legally or not) and the Right sees more cheap labor to exploit. Our immigration laws are not being vigorously enforced because politicians and their corporate sponsors on *both sides* want them in. The Left wants a microcosm of planet earth instead of a melting pot. The Right wants willing hands for jobs Americans supposedly won't do and "smart people" to create jobs here. (as if we don't have "smart people" here) By refusing to enforce our border security and immigration laws, particularly after the events of September 11, 2001, this government is discredited in the eyes of many

Americans. Allowing more immigrants in when the country has double digit unemployment and underemployment just doesn't make sense.

Despite *consistently* strong public support for tight border security and tough restrictions on all forms of immigration, our government has refused to carry out the demands of the people. Empty voting booths contribute to the defiance of our will. The politicians check on the latest polls, but they know the percentages change when a question is worded differently. They know the passage of time can cool emotions and like all statistics, the numbers can be manipulated depending on the special interest group or media network that produces the results. But our vote on election day still commands their attention and respect. It is our power to hire, rehire and fire our politicians. Sadly, the majority is rarely heard on election day, which has handed power to activists and extremists on both sides of the political spectrum. The voice of moderation has been drowned out by the jeers of fanatics on the Left and Right.

It seems like the moderate majority has given up on the system because there is little or no faith in these politicians who buy elections, who promise so much and deliver nothing. A democratic government is on thin ice if it does not have the consent of the majority and illegitimate if it is controlled by lobbyists who represent corporations and flag burning revolutionaries who despise their own country.

The primary responsibility of all federal, state and local politicians is the well being of their jurisdiction. The private sector can't do all of the work, our government has a significant role to play. Businesses must be regulated, taxes collected, roads repaired and laws enforced, etc. Universal registration plays a vital role, with it, we direct the course of government by electing people who support our political stance. We must take a hard look at the candidate and his/her political views. What is his past voting record? How does he stand on the issues important to you?

Do *you* really want more of these inheritance cases, lawyers, media darlings and coat tail cases in control?

Many elections ultimately represent a minority of the voter population. The turnouts are consistently low, from mayoral and sheriffs elections to the senatorial and presidential ones. There are many theories for this apathy. Some point to inconvenience and education. Age is also a factor, the elderly and middle-aged are far more likely to vote than young Americans. How about lack of faith in the people running? The American people are not as stupid as our government believes, many Americans have a firm grasp of the political process and are disgusted with the never ending corruption and out of step decision making. I'm talking about rich lawyers who can get even richer and they'll promise the world to reach that lofty, public office. Once they're elected, the promises are forgotten and they bow down to the left-wing and corporate interest groups that pull their strings.

The jurisdictional responsibilities are also forgotten. Obsessed with international events and global markets, our politicians are constantly sticking their snouts into the affairs of independent countries, intervening on behalf of foreign hordes for expanded freedoms and jobs. The effort and resources used for foreign handouts would be better spent on American citizens. Who do they think they are? If you're an American senator or representative, you have no legal authority off of American soil. The United States must stop behaving like the American Empire.

Can the Russian Duma change our speed

limits? Can Iranian policemen come here and place Americans under arrest? The answer to both is obviously no. But we would certainly resent a foreign politician dictating to us how we should live our lives. When someone is granted political power at any level, its limitations and jurisdiction must be respected. Its duties must be upheld to the best of ones ability, (like any job) but only to the individuals who bestowed this power upon you. The governor of California has no authority over the people of Connecticut and vice versa. Once a politician leaves his jurisdiction, his power is no more, because he is no longer within the area where popular consent was administered, no authority where it is not legally recognized.

For now, America is still the mightiest nation, therefore our government has a stronger influence in the world than any other. But our government is hated around the world because its policies increasingly reflect the interests of the military-industrial complex, greedy corporations and radicals. It is viewed as an out of control tyrant, not only in the Islamic world, but in Europe and Latin America as well. But this tyrant will never break the spirit of the American people. We can recreate it, so it will again do *our bidding,* disciplined and steadfast in its proper service to America. We can sweep away the corrupt and restore moderation and sense in government. We must stop these fools before we lose our country completely.

Our tax dollars are squandered by politicians with little regard for wise budgeting and responsible spending because it isn't their money. Over budget programs, inefficient transportation systems, an ongoing health care crisis, runaway trade deficits and foreign aid handouts have eaten away at our economy. Our government worries about disaster relief for Indonesia, Haiti and Pakistan, but they can't rebuild our own dams and bridges. They worry about feeding people in other countries when they should only worry about feeding millions of hungry people right here in the U.S.A. They worry about employing millions of unemployed in other countries when they should only worry about employing millions of unemployed and underemployed here.

It is not our responsibility to employ the world. It is not our responsibility to feed the world. The humanitarian aid spent abroad (banked by dictators) is not invested here because the government and their corporate sponsors want us to work for our food. Besides, from their cozy offices they don't see the need for it, because we supposedly don't have problems like that. Apparently, it's just too much for Washington to confront, that we actually have starving people in the United States.

Our country has an enormous tax base and our wallets, purses and paychecks are plundered for trillions of dollars, but we always hear about the country being broke and trillions in the hole. The politicians know the American people despise taxes and to protect their careers, they have to come up with good reasons to increase them. Paying "our debt" is viewed as an important priority by the people, so many would accept a tax increase on the condition that the money raised will truly diminish it. Improving schools and roads are other goals that require tax increases. But as all Americans should know, the revenue seldom goes where the politicians promise.

We are told that our deficits remain enormous and we can see for ourselves that our roads and schools remain the same. What are they doing with all of our money? The "official figures" released to the media boasting about job creation, lower unemployment, improved infrastructure and better schools can easily be doctored for our consumption by the people responsible for the condition of our economy, transportation and educational systems. These official looking documents and reports should not be automatically believed.

When the press asks a well rehearsed politician or spokesperson a direct question about the state of the economy or a political scandal, we rarely see direct and honest answers. "To the best of my knowledge, no information is available." "I have no recollection of that." "I have not been briefed on that." How many times have we heard this nonsense before? Sometimes, the official will acknowledge the question and with eyes blinking wildly, he/she will ramble on about a topic that has nothing to do with the question asked. Even with the Freedom of Information Act, we only learn from the government and its bureaucracy what they want us to know. If the country had a 15% unemployment rate, we would be told that the economy is entering a "cooling cycle." We're often told that crime rates are dropping, but why is the prison/probation population rising? Their numbers rarely add up or make sense.

In the real world, crime is out of control in much of the country and you don't have to read about another school or workplace shooting to understand that. Our police officers have to deal with tidal waves of thieves, perverts, murderers, illegal aliens, drunks and junkies. They have to deal with dangerous and frustrating situations to keep us safe. But they have to protect us with one hand tied behind their backs because of thin budgets and a touchy-feely justice system (the convict wasn't held enough) that puts the rights of the criminal above the rights of the victim and the public.

You know the areas of your own city that are unsafe and the neighborhoods that are neglected slums. Perhaps you have personally experienced violent crime. But we're told that our streets are secure and the governor or mayor will boast about reduced crime (armed with more reports and numbers) to bolster his re-election campaign, claiming that "his crime fighting strategies" worked wonders in his jurisdiction.

Exaggerations are also directed toward economic performance. The government or pro-business lobby may claim 9% unemployment; that is, 9% are on welfare or unemployment insurance.

But what about the people who exhausted their unemployment benefits and didn't find a job? They simply *disappear.* What about the millions

of underemployed and temporary workers regis-
tered with an agency still waiting for an assign-
ment? How many jobs were shipped overseas
and how many were forced to take a job that pays
less than the last one? What about the millions
more who work for minimum or near minimum
wage? So you see, the official unemployment rate
does not show the real hardships endured by our
workforce.

In addition, hundreds of thousands reluctantly
turn to bankruptcy to escape crushing debts. But
we always hear about how good things are and
how spoiled we are, so the nonsense continues.
But in the real world, statistics don't mean a lot.
What really matters are wages, prices and taxes.
We know which one of these isn't growing and
we know the other two are always rising.

All forms of public assistance, social security and unemployment insurance are financed
by the taxpaying American worker. Every payday
substantial deductions are made from our gross
earnings to ensure that in the event of some future
misfortune such as the loss of a job, injury or long
term illness, these programs will be readily available. After all, we pay for them and the banks
and landlords don't care if you're injured or out of

work, they just see numbers, not human beings. Unfortunately, street savvy cons, illegal aliens and program parasites reap the rewards too, leaving productive citizens with empty pockets and promises.

When a worker is seriously injured on the job, he is supposedly covered by federal, state and employer protection. The injured worker should expect medical treatment and compensation until he has recuperated sufficiently to return to work right? It's supposed to work this way, but there are obstacles. Immediately after the injury occurs, the employer can put pressure on the worker to prevent him/her from filing a claim. With a smile, management will tell the injured worker that they're not running a charity house in so many words and demand his swift return to the job. They can blame the mishap on the worker, claiming that "safety procedures were not followed." The employer can demand a drug/alcohol test on the employee and if any is detected, (no matter how small or how long ago it was taken) the employer can wash his hands of the incident and refuse to accept any financial or moral responsibility for it.

If these tactics do not succeed in derailing

the employee's intention of going ahead with a claim or lawsuit, the employer can drop rumors about finding a replacement and smear the injured worker's reputation at work. That's why intimidated workers are on the job with casts, bad backs, crushed fingers and aching teeth. They're not supposed to be working at all, but because of government stonewalling and employer bullying, they're suffering cruelly. There are workers on crutches and in wheelchairs performing "light duty" assignments and people who should be recovering from surgeries, child birth and kidney stones prematurely yanked out of their homes and hospital beds and put right back to work.

At the unemployment office, the methods are different, but also effective. Even when the unemployment is caused by a layoff or unjustified termination, there can be blatant resistance to getting the benefits. First, you have to qualify at all. You must have hundreds of hours of work within a calendar year or quarter. Each state has confusing base requirements and waiting periods. These stipulations eliminate thousands of workers from collecting a dime. Next, the employer has the right to intervene and block the benefits by furnishing its own story (fabricated or otherwise) about the events that led to loss of employment. If you successfully hurdle these obstacles and benefits are finally granted, the next phase begins. You must provide proof to the unemployment office that you are searching for new employment on demand. They can call your home and request the names and phone numbers of businesses that you applied with. If your search is deemed unsatisfactory, benefits can be immediately cut off.

The workers keep the entire system running and America's success depends on us, not the elite. With our work, we feed the rich and with our taxes, we feed the government and the poor. The nation is only as strong as its workforce. It is time to tax those who can afford to pay, it is time for the 200k club and up to pay for more working family tax breaks and higher wages. A strong working/middle class will provide the *incentive* for the poor to become workers themselves. $12 an hour jobs may be family wage jobs in Guatemala or India, but this is America. It was a decent wage in the 1970s, but in the 21st century, no one can get ahead or start a family on these earnings.

Just as a business is required to report its sales and profits to the government and investors, it should also report to its workforce with the same financial statements. People are often left in the dark about the *real success* of the company they work for, which results in management fiction that the business is unable to pay higher wages, when in fact it can. We must remember that many businesses would never exist at all without the loans and expertise provided by our government. But the owner quickly forgets about that when it starts turning a profit and he'll whine about "too much government regulation." Suddenly, it's all his, he "built the business by himself." When in fact, our tax dollars, work and government (S.B.A.) made his dream a reality. Without the infrastructure, expertise and labor, the entrepreneur is just another dreamer.

Wages have to be increased to restore the American nuclear family, which has taken a pounding for decades. Preaching about "family values" is not enough. Politicians have to fight on our behalf for *family wage jobs* too. This country is not just about business, it is about families. Our tax structure must shift more of the burden to multi-nationals and millionaires. Wasteful spending, senseless wars, foreign aid handouts and corruption can be controlled and eliminated with an efficient, fair government. If not, then politicians must be replaced and punished just like any other citizen and held fully accountable for their actions or inactions.

We need people in government who comprehend the challenges that face the American worker everyday, people who understand what it's like to work for a living. Too many of our representatives, senators and governors were filthy rich before they even ran for office. No more snobs and inheritance cases. Too many of them side with the rich when they're elected and lose any concern (if they had any from the start) for the workers and the poor.

Our country is like a ship in an angry sea. The vessel is being tossed and turned by the crashing waves and howling winds. The people on board below are the workers and they're doing their best to repair damage and plug the leaks. The people above in the bridge are the politicians and the rich. These few decide what course the ship will take. Later that day, the storm begins to subside and the vessel is intact. However, due to gross incompetence, the ship slams into a reef offshore and begins to breakup on the jagged rocks. The ship is lost at sea because of the people in control of it. The crew is blameless, they followed their orders and were exemplary in their execution, but they were helpless to prevent the disaster because they had no control over the situation. The blame is on the people in the bridge. You have to point the finger at the people *in control.*

America has had its fair share of great leaders, men and women who have enhanced its power and led it to victory over formidable adversaries. At the presidential level, Washington, Jefferson, Theodore Roosevelt, Franklin Roosevelt, Truman and Eisenhower come to mind for many Americans.

With their wisdom and courage, they helped to build the foundations, establish its institutions, protect its borders and guide it in times of domestic and foreign crisis. But in more recent times, Americans have lived under presidents that history will certainly judge as mediocre or ineffective. Voters refer to their reluctant choice as the "lesser of two evils." Enthusiasm has dampened for our political candidates. Today's leaders are viewed as out of touch with our needs. Special interest groups have seemingly diluted concern and dedication for the well being of our country. Corruption scandals have damaged trust and with that decline in trust, respect is diminished.

If someone has little or no respect for politicians, then why have any more for the laws and regulations they create and enforce? Leadership begins at the top and if incompetence is shown here, the rot will pollute the middle and lower levels of government and the bureaucracy. It is absolutely necessary for the figures at the top to set a good example for the rest, so the government machine can function for the benefit of its citizens without being tainted by bribery and indecisiveness.

Boasting about doing God's work while giving tax breaks to the rich is contradictory. Look at your own life and ask yourself if you have benefited from the good rule of our political leaders. Politicians don't have haloes above their heads and we shouldn't have a childlike trust in their ability to solve all our problems, but government is necessary and we should trust that the powers we give them will not be abused.

You are a human being with great potential and a unique purpose. You are aware of your limitations and weaknesses, we all have them. But concentrate now on your strengths and capabilities. Think about what you want to accomplish and where you want to be in the near future. Are you disappointed and frustrated with your current position and status? Are you reluctant to face the truth head on? Or do you immerse yourself in television and fantasy, cling to *unrealistic* optimism or dream of winning the lottery? The respectable level of success that you hope, work and pray for can be elusive or impossible when you're working so hard to make the dreams of the rich come true instead. You're not alone. You're one among millions who are being used to fatten the bellies and bank accounts of a few. Is this what God intended for you? Surely there is more to life than that.

If you are employed, pay taxes and obey the laws, then you are essentially playing by the rules of the game. But if all you have for playing by the system's rules is debt and unsatisfying living standards, then you are losing this game. It's late in the third quarter and the score is: System 28 and Worker 3. But you and I don't pass laws, increase taxes or regulate business. Our government is responsible for these actions in our name.

Corporations can not be allowed to buy their actions. The rich can not be allowed to use our government to create and enforce an economy that suits them at the expense of the vast majority. Our major political parties are failing us, falling far short of defending real opportunity for all Americans. Supply side economics that give free rides to the rich are not the answer. They are richer than ever, but your future is not in their hands. To accomplish this, wages have shrunk and unions busted to enhance their profits. Workers have paid the price and the rich are laughing all the way to the bank.

Our government must enforce, not attack workers rights. The humane course that began with the New Deal must continue. But that role has been weakened and the workers are again under the whip of the rich. If these greedy, power mad millionaires and billionaires get their way, we will have a corporate government, all union power will be abolished and we will work for bread.

History has shown what the rich have done (and will do again) to increase their profits. Americans have been enslaved and murdered for striking, for wanting a better life. Who in their right mind supports a plutocratic America? This is our democracy at stake.

As usual, the poor have seen no improvements as more among their ranks turn to crime to survive. They can make more by stealing cars, mugging people and selling drugs. There is little incentive to get a job when so many offer pathetic wages.

The government and Wall Street expect people to make large purchases like houses and new cars and splurge during the holidays with no job security or no job at all. People simply can't take these financial risks when their job can be instantly outsourced or they're not well connected with the powers that be of the employer. By diminishing wages and outsourcing jobs, the elite have destroyed the very foundation of our economy, which depends on consumer spending and confidence.

Melting Pot or Melting Not

America's illegal immigration problem is nothing new. People have sneaked into our country through the Canadian border, on ships crossing the Pacific Ocean and on leaky rafts crossing the Straits of Florida. But by far, the greatest threat to our territorial security is along the lengthy Mexican-American border. Illegal aliens continue to pour into our country, bringing a heavy financial burden to incarcerate, feed and deport them. After expulsion, he will attempt to enter again and again. Millions have succeeded and typically work in landscaping, agriculture, restaurants, construction, or as house servants, while his employers turn a blind eye to his unlawful stay in our country. Next, the illegal alien can abuse our hospitality by claiming he has the "right" to become an American citizen.

Since when does anyone have the *right* to become an American citizen? Certainly, no foreigner has the right to break our laws without consequence. Becoming an American citizen is in fact, a *privilege* that can be granted or denied at our discretion, not the illegal alien's. An immigrant must knock on our door before entering our home and should only be allowed to enter by abiding by our rules. We do not have to open the door at all. If we allow entry, he must respect our laws or be thrown out. Illegals have chosen to break into our home instead and make themselves comfortable to our detriment.

But the government and the rich are not concerned. With a wink and a nod to illegals, (we won't punish you, we'll let you work) the defense of our borders is halfhearted and unacceptable. But the rich don't have to live in their ghettos and love to take advantage of them. The illegals will wash dishes, mow lawns and pick apples for minimum wage or less. The rich are never satisfied with American productivity anyway, they think we're lazy and spoiled. So the aliens are an easy, illegal way to boost their bottom lines. Here is yet another example of what the rich will do to increase their profits.

If the federal government got serious about protecting our borders and stopping the flow of illegals, it could provide funding for cement and surveillance and build walls or reinforce the border patrol with our army and impose lengthy prison sentences on illegal aliens and their employers. Of course, these are tough measures, but they are all within our government's power. Moreover, it has a duty to do so, to defend our sovereignty and punish tax evaders. Politicians who throw their hands in the air and say nothing can be done about border defense are liars and they should be removed from office.

Many Americans would not have a problem with people entering our home if they did so *legally*. Then we can have the opportunity to screen them and find out what their intentions are once they enter. But by sneaking in, we can't help but wonder, what is he hiding? Drugs? A violent criminal record? A terror plot? Unfortunately, our government does little more than pay election time lip service to this critical issue. Politicians scramble to garner immigrant votes and stronger border security will obviously produce the opposite effect.

Liberals and conservatives have their uses for

illegal aliens (future votes, cheap labor) that have been placed above border security and public safety.

Americans are also wondering how people arrive here penniless and functionally illiterate and then all of a sudden, they're studying to be doctors and engineers in our finest colleges. Others arrive and suddenly, they take over the corner convenience stores and motels in the community. Meanwhile, many of our hardest working and intelligent citizens can only dream about a college degree or business ownership and fail to qualify for the same government assistance that the immigrant enjoys. There is also the myth that they work harder than Americans. They do not, but they will work for less, which has contributed to the stagnation of our wages. If we won't work for low wages, there are plenty of immigrants available who will. The government also looks at the immigrants as "fresh blood" for the nation and more future heads to tax.

Our increasingly diverse, multi-cultural society is facing the same challenges as failed multi-cultural nations of the past like Austria-Hungary, Yugoslavia and the Soviet Union. These deceased nations consisted of many nationalities that were often at odds with each other. They were bound together by exaggerated outside threats, propaganda and force. All three of them perished in 75 years or less.

Austria-Hungary was a mixed up collection of Germans, Hungarians, Serbs, Croats, Slovaks, Slovenes, Poles, Ukrainians, Romanians, Italians, Gypsies and Muslims. Its neighbors were Germany, Italy, Romania, Serbia and Russia. Austria-Hungary's restless minorities often worked for unification with their ethnic homelands just over the border. There were Germans who wanted to secede and merge with the German state. There were Serbs who wanted to break with Austria and join with Serbia and Italians who wanted unification with Italy. These nationalist pressures caused tremendous strain on the moribund empire and it was a daily challenge to keep it together. A flag was not enough. During World War I, Austria-Hungary went to war with Italy, Serbia and Romania and the loyalties of its Italian, Serb and Romanian minorities were always in doubt.

After the disintegration of Austria-Hungary in 191 8, Yugoslavia emerged as a hasty compromise to provide stability in the region. Many of the former Austrian territories were lumped together, containing Serbia, Croatia, Bosnia-Herzegovina, Montenegro and Slovenia. Its diverse population was held together by brute force under Tito's communist dictatorship until 1980. The country swiftly unraveled in the 1990s resulting in a bloody struggle for land among Serbs, Croats and Muslims. There was no common language, faith or identity to preserve it. Old ethnic hatred literally tore the country apart.

The Soviet Union was home for Russians, Belorussians, Ukrainians, Armenians, Tatars, Kazakhs, Turkmen, Georgians, Azerbaijanis, Uzbeks and many other Muslim and indigenous people who rarely got along. The Soviet government resorted to harsh measures and suffocating propaganda that promoted unrealistic visions of these many ethnic groups molded into one, the Soviet People. The regime faced a political challenge when it invaded Muslim Afghanistan in 1979 and Soviet atrocities against Afghan citizens had to be concealed from the USSR's large Muslim population. A striking similarity involves America's wars in Iraq and Afghanistan. The many ethnic groups of the Soviet Union lived together because they were forced to by a totalitarian regime. It was not a voluntary union. With

Gorbachev's reforms came the speedy collapse of this multi-cultural union.

As a multi-cultural state, America's 21st century fortunes will depend on its race relations. If more cracks appear in the American mortar, its citizens can expect more propaganda and politically correct standardization to sustain it. Those who choose to remain exclusively with their own people, to worship the same God (or gods) and share a similar history and culture could be branded as racists and xenophobes. Those who point out that multi-cultural societies have a poor stability and longevity record will require "sensitivity training."

The elite have trusted in the nation's future as a multi-cultural, multi-religious and multi-lingual society by giving citizenship to foreigners and encouraging them to use their abilities for their benefit and America's. But this certainly doesn't prove that every foreigner who enters the country is gifted and beneficial to our society. This fact has put tremendous strain on our courts, prisons, educational systems and social programs to accommodate these new arrivals. The costs are passed off to the American taxpayer, who is ineligible to receive the same social and educational benefits.

The victim is the born in America taxpayer, who is expected to provide, but not receive, the comforts of pampered citizenship. All too often, our country is viewed as a convenient host (not a beloved home) for quick money or an education that can be exploited or discarded when convenient.

In that run down district of your city, you will see a preview of the darkening future awaiting this country. It used to be a good neighborhood, but now the buildings have deteriorated, the yards are unkempt and the schools have declined. The transformation was swift, property values sank and crime increased. The destruction of our cities is a cancer spreading into the suburbs and wrecking the hard work of its residents. They reluctantly sell their homes and move away from the invaders, run out of their own community by illegal hordes. Local businesses follow suit, creating a dual effect of lost tax revenues and employment for the city. The result, an area bloated with crime and filth, inhabited by thugs who wander the streets. More invaders settle in and reproduce like rabbits, ensuring future welfare and more conquered neighborhoods.

The "invisible hand" of the free market will fix this right? Just dump more immigrants into the ghettos and a few of them will get laundry mats and gas stations opened. Then investment will return and the community will thrive again! The glass is still half full in these destroyed neighborhoods packed with poverty and racism, there is always hope.

The obstacles that stymie American multi-cultural harmony involve much more than traditional black-white racism. Of course, these relations are important and there have been obvious improvements since the race riots and turmoil of the 1960s. However, the same hostile attitudes still exist and they're not confined to the southern United States. You will find them in the northern U.S. too, they're just not as blatant, since the Ku Klux Klan, post-Civil War Jim Crow laws, lynching and the Confederacy itself are automatically identified with the southern states.

It is interesting to note that as long as the great majority of blacks resided in the southern (Confederate) states, the northern abolitionist movement worked vigorously to end slavery and grant equal rights to them. That is, as long as they stayed in the South. It was easy to support a cause when it was far from home. But with substantial black migration to the northern states following the war, came widespread hostility toward them, as northern whites were forced to compete with the new arrivals for housing and employment.

The segregation of whites and minorities is just as obvious in northern cities as in southern ones. America's greatest city is the largest example. New York has experienced continuous ethnic change, as new immigrants have moved in and old ones have been run out. The first population change was from Dutch to English. The second was from English to German and Irish. These groups were eclipsed by Italians and Jews by 1900. By 1945, these groups were competing with a growing black and Puerto Rican population. This trend continued and along with Arab, Asian and Dominican immigration, New York was transformed from a 2/3 majority city into a 2/3 minority one.

The Bronx is primarily Hispanic today, with a few pockets of black and Italian neighborhoods. Manhattan is predominantly white and Asian until you go north of 125th Street. From that point up to Washington Heights is black Harlem and Spanish Harlem. In Brooklyn and Queens, there are exclusively Italian, Jewish and black areas, as well as Irish, Puerto Rican, Chinese, Dominican,

Russian, Ukrainian and Arab. The city is not integrated at all and there have always been bitter rivalries among its various ethnic groups. Besides an occasional riot, police shooting or discrimination lawsuit, these tensions rarely make the news. But it's an everyday fact of life for New York residents because the tension is on the street, in the schools, subways and bus stops. Obviously, these groups prefer to have their own areas and inter-ethnic conflicts are rooted in economic competition. As long as people make money and have their own "turf" the structure will hold, but when a new group pours into a traditionally settled neighborhood and tries to "take over", tensions increase.

In America's growing Hispanic population, there are some disturbing attitudes, particularly among Mexicans and Puerto Ricans. A common attitude among Puerto Ricans is that Mexicans give them a bad name or reputation. The illegal immigration and poverty of Mexico can offend the Puerto Rican when he/she is mistakenly identified as Mexican. For many Americans, it is difficult to distinguish one from the other, so both groups are commonly identified as Mexican, due to their much greater numbers. In fact, there are significant differences between them. While Mexico and Puerto Rico are both former Spanish colonies, Spanish speaking and predominantly Roman Catholic, over 70% of Mexicans are of Spanish-Amerindian descent (mestizo) while over 70% of Puerto Ricans are of European descent. (Spanish, Italian, German, French) Some Puerto Ricans also have African, Lebanese and Chinese ancestry. Puerto Rico is far more Americanized than Mexico due to its U.S. Commonwealth status. Thus, when a Puerto Rican moves from San Juan to New York or Orlando, he feels that he is home. The Puerto Rican may view the Mexican as an invader. On the other hand, the Mexican may view the Puerto Rican as spoiled and partially Anglocized. When the Mexican moves from Guadalajara to San Antonio, he feels that he is home too, since Texas, Califronia, Arizona and Nevada were until 1848, Mexican territory.

Rivalry within the Hispanic population is rooted in the inequalities of the caste system of the Spanish Empire.

This system was based on race. At the top were European born whites, followed by colonial born whites, people of mixed Spanish-Indian ancestry, (mestizos) Spanish-black ancestry, (mulattoes) native Indians and Africans.

Anti-semitic attitudes exist in America and should increase as the Arab/muslim population increases. Greeks and Armenians have a long history of hatred for Turks. Native Indians, who are of Asian origin, will never forget the conquest of their lands and their near extermination at the hands of white colonial settlers, whether Spanish, French, English or American. The facts of history can not be erased with sops and politically correct revisions.

Being white in America can present confusing classifications. Jews are generally white, but not Christian. Many Spaniards, Portuguese, Cubans, Puerto Ricans, Dominicans and Mexicans are mistaken for "Anglos." Being black in America can be equally confusing. Some prefer the terms African-American or Afro-American. But not all American blacks came here directly from Africa. Some arrived from Haiti, Jamaica, Dominican Republic, Trinidad and Tobago, Brazil and Cuba. Some of these people speak Spanish, so they may prefer to be classified as Hispanic. Some American blacks aren't black at all, their skin is light brown or even white, resulting in subtle light skin/dark skin racism. They've been known as negroes, coloreds, blacks, Afro-Americans and African-Americans.

We are told that "diversity is a strength." But in reality, our multi-cultural society is very difficult to deal with. There is always the risk of offending someone and the risk of fragmentation is real. With a current population of over 310 million and an estimated population of 350 million by 2025, America is a saturated state. Runaway immigration will increase urban sprawl, energy consumption and destruction to our environment. It is time for America to slam the door on illegal immigration and strictly enforce limited, *legal immigration*.

We have to focus on our own enormous problems and repair corporate abuses.

The jobs must be kept in America and we need politicians to turn voter demands into reality.

But if corporations and the idle rich are allowed to retain their stranglehold on our economy, the canyon between the wealthy and working poor will keep widening and our great country will be reduced to a noble and peasant society. Old ethnic tensions will rise and America could face dissolution.

If the radical Left and PC speech police are

allowed to continue their assault on our social values, our freedoms of religion and speech will be seriously threatened. Our military and criminal justice system will soften and be too feeble to defend our borders and protect the public from criminals. More hordes of illegal immigrants will be allowed into the country, transforming the American Southwest into Northern Mexico.

The path of moderation will ensure our country's survival, but the longer we delay, the greater the damage will be to our economy, social discipline and optimism. The time is now.